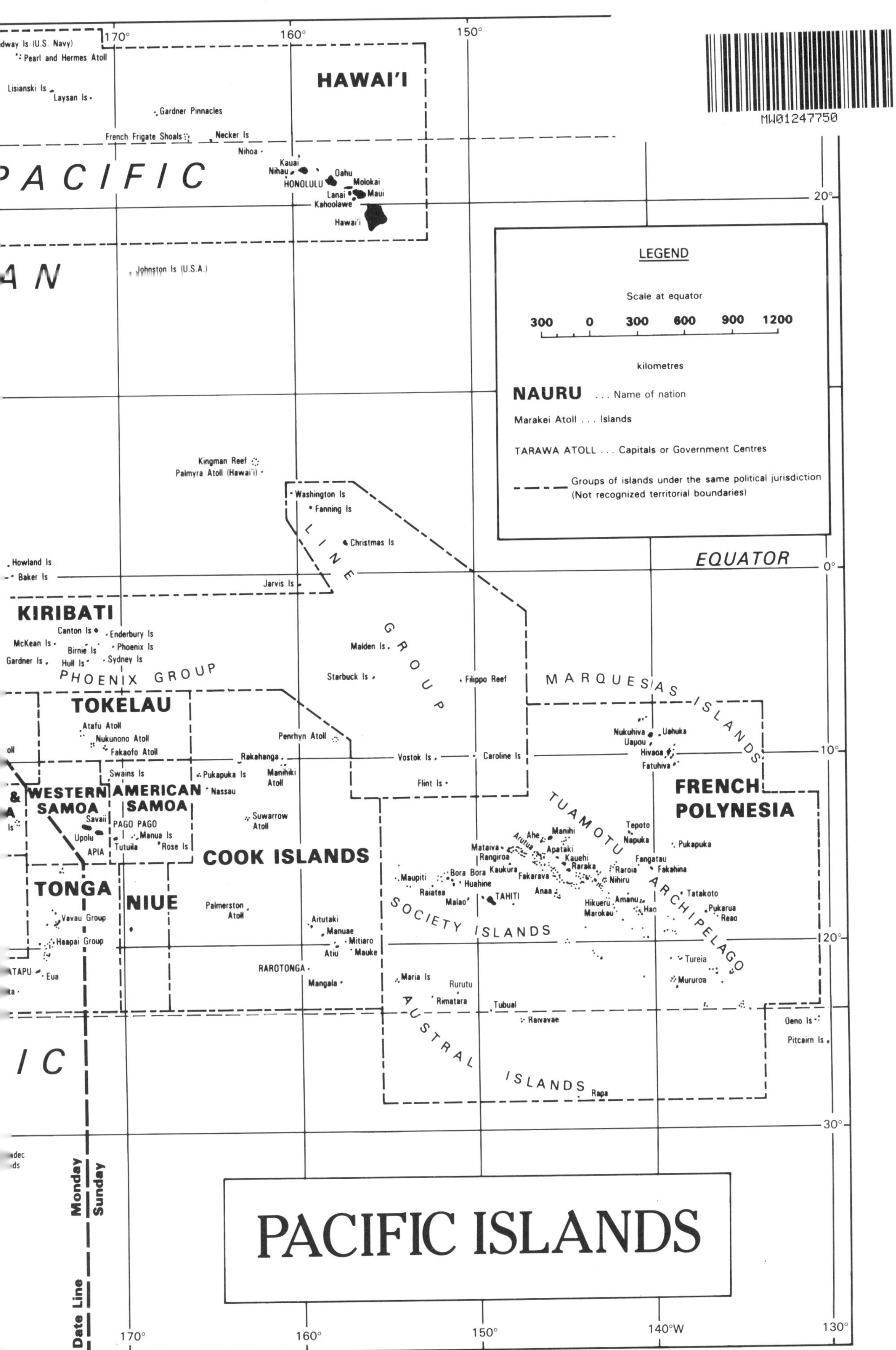

PACIFIC ISLANDS
LEGEND
Scale at equator
300 0 300 600 900 1200
kilometres
NAURU ... Name of nation
Marakei Atoll ... Islands
TARAWA ATOLL ... Capitals or Government Centres
Groups of islands under the same political jurisdiction (Not recognized territorial boundaries)
HAWAI'I
Pearl and Hermes Atoll
Lisianski Is
Laysan Is
Gardner Pinnacles
French Frigate Shoals
Necker Is
Nihoa
Kauai
Niihau
Oahu
HONOLULU
Molokai
Lanai
Maui
Kahoolawe
Hawai'i
PACIFIC
Johnston Is (U.S.A.)
Kingman Reef
Palmyra Atoll (Hawai'i)
Washington Is
Fanning Is
Christmas Is
LINE GROUP
Jarvis Is
Malden Is
Starbuck Is
Filippo Reef
EQUATOR
Howland Is
Baker Is
KIRIBATI
Canton Is
Enderbury Is
McKean Is
Birnie Is
Phoenix Is
Gardner Is
Hull Is
Sydney Is
PHOENIX GROUP
TOKELAU
Atafu Atoll
Nukunono Atoll
Fakaofo Atoll
Swains Is
WESTERN SAMOA
AMERICAN SAMOA
Savaii
Upolu
APIA
PAGO PAGO
Manua Is
Tutuila
Rose Is
Penrhyn Atoll
Rakahanga
Pukapuka Is
Manihiki Atoll
Nassau
Suwarrow Atoll
COOK ISLANDS
Vostok Is
Caroline Is
Flint Is
MARQUESAS ISLANDS
Nukuhiva
Uahuka
Uapou
Hivaoa
Fatuhiva
FRENCH POLYNESIA
TUAMOTU ARCHIPELAGO
Tepoto
Napuka
Pukapuka
Ahe
Manihi
Arutua
Apataki
Mataiva
Rangiroa
Kauehi
Raraka
Kaukura
Fakarava
Fangatau
Raroia
Fakahina
Nihiru
Maupiti
Bora Bora
Huahine
Raiatea
Malao
TAHITI
Anaa
Hikueru
Marokau
Amanu
Hao
Tatakoto
Pukarua
Reao
SOCIETY ISLANDS
Tureia
Mururoa
TONGA
NIUE
Vavau Group
Haapai Group
Eua
Palmerston Atoll
Aitutaki
Manuae
Mitiaro
Atiu
Mauke
RAROTONGA
Mangaia
Maria Is
Rurutu
Rimatara
Tubuai
Raivavae
AUSTRAL ISLANDS
Rapa
Oeno Is
Pitcairn Is
Monday
Sunday
Date Line
170°
160°
150°
140°W
130°
20°
10°
0°
30°

The Pacific in the 20th Century

Pacific People and Change

Max Quanchi

The right of the
University of Cambridge
to print and sell
all manner of books
was granted by
Henry VIII in 1534.
The University has printed
and published continuously
since 1584.

Cambridge University Press
Cambridge
New York Port Chester Melbourne Sydney

Published by the Press Syndicate of the University of Cambridge
The Pitt Building, Trumpington Street, Cambridge CB2 1RP, UK
40 West 20th Street, New York, NY 10011, USA
10 Stamford Road, Oakleigh, Melbourne 3166, Australia

First published 1991

Printed in Hong Kong by Colorcraft Ltd

National Library of Australia cataloguing-in-publication data

Quanchi, Max.
Pacific people and change.

Includes index.
ISBN 0 521 37627 0.

1. Islands of the Pacific — History — 20th century. I. Title.

990

Contents

Acknowledgements

The author would like to thank Andrew Thornley in Sydney, Martin Peake, Stephanie Fahey and Brigid James in Melbourne, and the many teachers and friends in the Pacific Islands who offered suggestions on various parts of the text. Thanks also to Jim Warburton and Gary Underwood for guiding the manuscript through to publication.

Grateful acknowledgement is made to the following for permission to reprint copyright material.

Allen & Unwin, Australia for *Where the Waves Fall*, K. R. Howe, 1984; Australian Museum for two figures from 'Melanesian Art in the Australian Museum', D. R. Moore & C. V. Turner, p. 10; Blond & Briggs, U.K. for *Treasure Island: the Trials of the Banabans*, P. Binder, 1977; Dodd Mead & Co., Publishers, USA, for *Hokule'a: the Way to Tahiti*, 1979, B. R. Finney; The *Bulletin*; Fiji Museum for *Drawings by Winifred Mumford*, author L. Birks; The Journal of Pacific History for maps from *Sea Level Changes and Pacific Prehistory* by J. Gibbons and F. Clunie, vol. 21: 1–2, p. 62; Millwood Press, N.Z. for Fig. 40 (Bruce Askew), Fig. 41 (J. Siers), Fig. 36 (L. Green) in *Taratai* by James Siers, 1977; Musée de L'homme, Paris for Lapita Designs; Douglas L. Oliver for *Bougainville: a Personal History (1973)*; W. W. Norton & Co. Inc. for map from *Pacific Destiny*, E. Hoyt, 1981; Dr Jens Poulsen for photographs of Lapita Pottery; Ronin Films; Routledge & Kegan Paul Ltd for *Migrating Myth and Magic from the Gilbert Islands*, 1972, Rosemary Grimble, illustrator; The University of Chicago Press for map in *Meaning and Struggle in a Resettled Pacific Community*, 1971 by Prof. M. Silverman (map adapted from *The Social Organisation of Banaba or Ocean Island, Central Pacific*, Journal of Polynesian Society, vol. 41, no. 4, 1932, pp. 262–30); University of Hawaii Press for maps from *Exiles & Migrants in Oceana* by Michael D. Leiber; University of the South Pacific, Institute of Pacific Studies for map in *Land Tenure in the Pacific*, 1977, R. Crocombe (ed.) and drawing in *Binabina: The Making of a Gela War Canoe*, 1983, R. T. Pule.

Quotations used in this text are from the following sources:

page 15: from V. Tausie *Art in the New Pacific*, Institute of Pacific Studies, University of the South Pacific, Suva, 1980, p. xv

page 27: from The *Sun* (Melbourne) 18 Feb, 1984

from The *Age* (Melbourne) 30 May, 1987

page 36: from *Pacific Islands Monthly* (50th Anniversary Special Edition), p. 181

from G. Souter *New Guinea: the Last Unknown*, Angus & Robertson, Melbourne, 1963, p. 181

pages 37 & 38: from the soundtrack of *First Contact*, a film by R. Anderson and B. Connelly, 1983

page 48: from V. Pitakaka 'Gilbertese in Titiana' in Ben Waita *et al.*, *Land in the Solomon Islands*, Institute of Pacific Studies, University of the South Pacific, Suva, 1979, p. 146

pages 50 & 61: from the soundtrack of *Angels of War*, a film by H. Nelson, A. Pike & G. Daws, Ronan Films, Canberra, 1984

page 50: from K. F. Koch (ed.) *Logs in the Current of the Sea*, Australian National University Press, Canberra, 1978, p. 28

page 54: from H. Nelson 'When foreigners battle on other people's fields; the impact of World War II on Papua New Guinea', unpublished paper presented at the HTAV (History Teachers' Association of Victoria) Conference, Marysville, 1986, p. 7

page 62: from H. Laracy (ed.) *Tuvalua: a History*, Institute of Pacific Studies, University of the South Pacific, Suva, 1976, p. 144

pages 71 & 73: from B. Finney *Hokule'a: the Way to Tahiti*, Dodd Mead & Co., New York, 1979, p. 271

page 73: from D. Lewis *From Maui to Cook*, Doubleday, Sydney, 1977, pp. 202–4

page 74: from *Pacific Islands Monthly*, June, 1980

page 77: from R. T. Pule *Binabina: the Making of a Gela War Canoe*, Institute of Pacific Studies, University of the South Pacific, Suva, 1983, p. 36

Every effort has been made to trace and acknowledge copyright but in some cases this has not been possible.

Introduction

This is one of three books in the series **The Pacific in the 20th Century**. They have been specifically written for middle secondary students. Each of the three books in the series examines a different aspect of the Pacific. *Pacific People and Place* covers the geography of the islands and issues related to development. *Pacific People and Change* covers key events and changes occurring in the recent history of the islands. *Pacific People and Society* examines issues which affect individuals, groups and communities in the islands.

At a time when people everywhere are trying to learn more about the islands and peoples of the Pacific, this series of books takes an important step forward in increasing our level of understanding and in combating ignorance of one of the major regions of the world.

Pacific People and Change traces the origins of the people of the Pacific through the archaeological evidence only recently being uncovered. This is history, not in the form of printed words and books, but in the form of pottery, sea-level changes, canoe designs, art, oral myths and legends.

Physical changes have occurred both many years ago and in the recent past in the Pacific and the people have been forced to respond to these changes. A chapter on volcanic activity demonstrates this quite clearly. Changes in human behaviour have also occurred, but the ancient traditions of the people of the Pacific can still be traced to more recent events in the 20th century. The voyage of the *Hokule'a* and the art of the Abelam people demonstrate the links between the past and the present. The story of the Phoenix Island and Solomon Islands migrations of the Kiribati people demonstrate this continuing pattern of adaptation, mobility and the adoption of new and useful ideas. The history of the Pacific in the 20th century also shows that human behaviour followed a different pattern when outside influences came to the islands. The recent meeting of Highlanders and explorers in Papua New Guinea and the experiences of Islanders caught in a combat war zone, demonstrate how Islanders were sometimes changed by outside influences, but also how they usually maintained both their old ways and what they found useful in the new.

In the last twenty years a further change has occurred as Pacific people have sought to reassert their identity. This has taken two directions: a search for the past through recreating the food and clothing, constructions, voyaging, dancing and story-telling of their ancestors; and a second struggle to assert land rights, national sovereignty and independence. The story of the Banaban people is only one example of how Pacific people are using new ways to solve age-old problems.

This history of the people of the Pacific has been written for students who want to learn about the Pacific. These students will find that this book offers a view of the Pacific from the other side — a history of the Pacific which focuses on the aspirations, emotions and actions of Pacific Islanders, rather than on the European strangers and visitors who stayed momentarily or passed by briefly.

The inquiry approach has been used and each chapter follows the same pattern. Students are asked to work their way through a series of activities designed to test an initial assumption or proposition. Each chapter ends with the student being asked to review and reflect upon these early guesses.

One of the aims of this book is to develop an appreciation of the craft of the historian, and within a general social science framework, to apply the skills and methodologies of the historian to questions about the Pacific in the 20th century. The initial focus question is followed by a brief introductory section and a list of related questions. These provide the student with a guide to the historical materials they will be working with later in the chapter. There are sets of questions and activities interspersed within the main body of the text. They have a sequential development, beginning with comprehension-based activities through to questions which require more logic and methodological development. There is a resource list at the end of each chapter which will assist students who wish to do further research.

A student's inquiry into the Pacific in the 20th century would benefit from several teacher-directed lessons, the screening of films, and visits by speakers planned for the purpose of offering alternative case studies or for providing greater depth of material on the issues raised in the text.

Max Quanchi

1

Clues to the Past: the Lapita Pottery Makers

Focus question

Were the Lapita pottery makers the ancestors of the first people to occupy Polynesia?

Caves, archaeology, pottery and history

A large cave, forty metres underwater, in a rock cliff on an atoll in Tuvalu in the central Pacific was explored by divers in 1986. In the cave the divers found stones, charcoal and signs of human occupation.

Two years later, archaeologists found a cave on New Ireland, an off-shore island north of Papua New Guinea. In this cave at Matenkupkum, they found shells and stones which had been flaked for use as tools. Laboratory tests indicated they were at least 33 000 years old.

These two caves are now the centre of attention in the long-running debate over the origins of the people of Polynesia.

At the time when people were using the cave in Tuvalu in the central Pacific it would have been above sea-level along a shoreline, or even higher up on a cliff overlooking a beach or reef. Sea-levels have risen gradually since the last great Ice Age which suggests that the occupiers of this cave were the first people to settle in Tuvalu as early as 8000 or 9000 years ago (called 9000 BP or *Before Present*). This suggestion has yet to be proved.

Archaeologists have shown already that around 4000 BP a group of sea-faring traders and settlers in Melanesia in the western Pacific developed an unusual style of pottery. This has been called Lapita pottery after the site in New Caledonia where it was first found. Some time after 4000 BP they carried this pottery with them eastwards into much of the Pacific. The date previously suggested for first settlement in Tuvalu was around 1200 AD. If the new findings are correct this date for Tuvalu will be pushed back 3000 years.

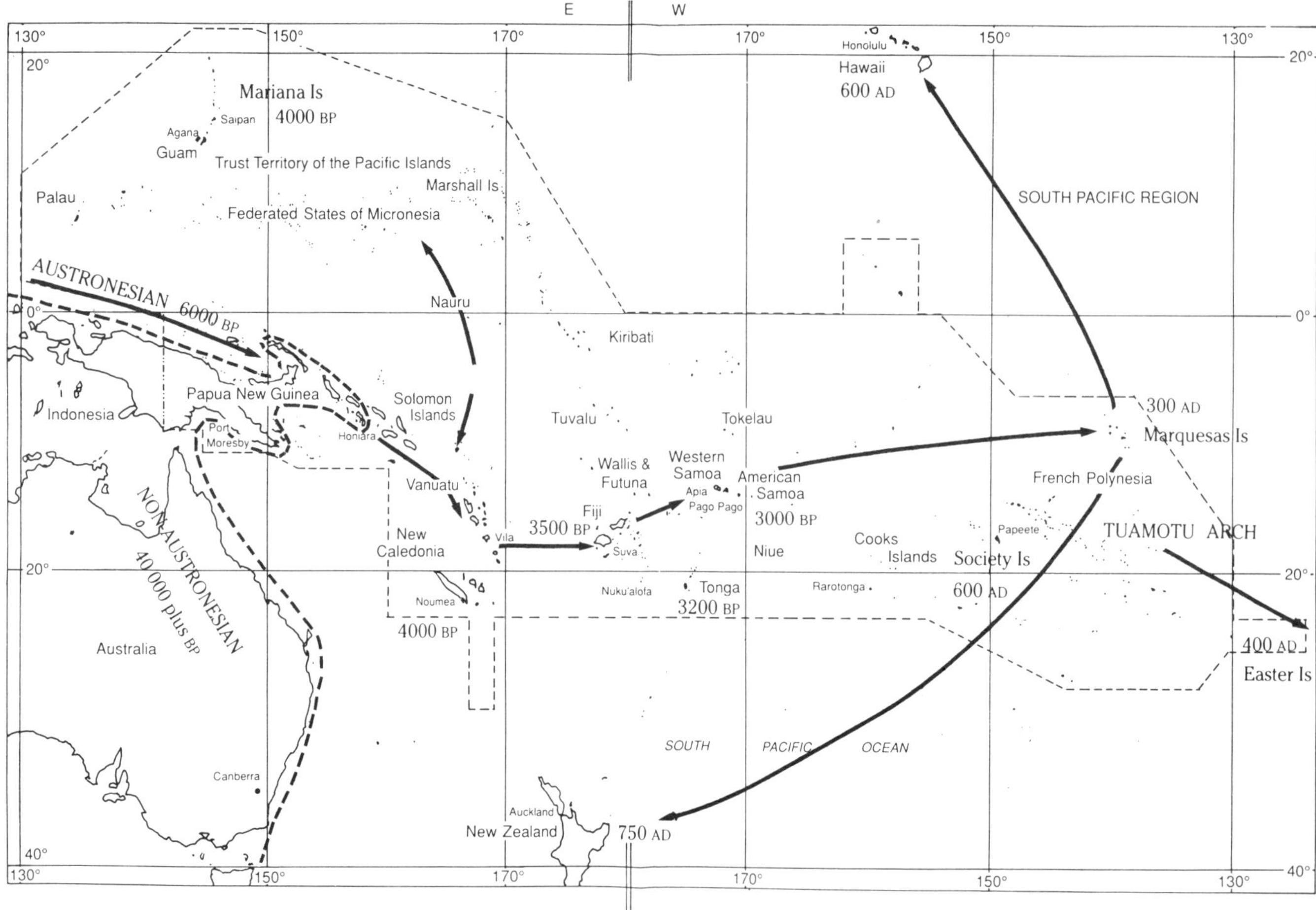

Fig. 1. Map of Pacific settlement. The arrows and dates are based on theories put forward in 1983.

For the last twenty years it has been accepted that the Lapita pottery makers from Melanesia were the ancestors of the traders, settlers and explorers who moved out to occupy the groups of islands now called Samoa, Tonga, Cook Islands, Marquesas and Society Islands, that is, Polynesia (meaning many islands). By 1600 BP the Lapita pottery makers had disappeared for reasons still unknown. It is also recognised that several aspects of modern eastern Pacific (Polynesian) culture and lifestyle are quite different from the lifestyle and culture of the western Pacific (Melanesian) people.

Before the discoveries and radio-carbon dating of artefacts from the Matenkupkum cave on New Ireland, it was believed that the first occupation of the offshore islands in Papua New Guinea was about 11 000 years ago. It is now suggested that this might have taken place 33 000 years ago. It is also being suggested that the Lapita potters were not the first to settle in Polynesia, and that the date for the first settlement in the eastern Pacific might be 5000 or more years earlier than is now accepted.

As each archaeological discovery is made, the early history (or pre-history) of Melanesia and Polynesia is therefore being rewritten.

Fig. 2. Lapita designs. Is this Lapita Decorated or Lapita Plainware style? Can you tell which incision technique was used to stamp the patterns on the pots?

▲▲▲ Related questions ▲▲▲

1 How do archaeologists contribute to the writing of history?

2 Where did Lapita pottery come from?

3 How did Lapita pottery spread throughout the Pacific?

4 Can archaeologists prove that people had occupied Polynesia before the Lapita potters arrived?

5 Can knowledge of changing sea-levels identify the time of arrival of the first Polynesians?

ACTIVITIES

1 Draw a big map, perhaps A3 size, of the Bismarck Archipelago. Only indicate the equator, north and the scale on it at this stage.

2 Write answers to these questions.
a What does an archaeologist do?
b What does an historian do?

3 Here are four facts. Read them and answer the following questions.
▲ In 1984 the historian Kerry Howe published a book, *Where the Waves Fall*, containing the following statement about Polynesians on the islands of Tonga. '. . . the Lapita seafarers ranged ever onward and had settled Tonga by about 3200 BP.'
▲ An underwater cave found in the islands of Tuvalu in Polynesia shows signs of human occupation from possibly 9000 BP.
▲ Pottery discoveries in Melanesia (New Caledonia, Solomon Islands, Vanuatu and Papua New Guinea) have only been dated as far back as 4000 BP.
▲ Artefacts, but no Lapita pottery, have been found in a cave at Missil in Melanesia (on New Britain Island) dated from 11 000 BP.
a When did Lapita pottery develop in Melanesia?
b When did the first occupiers of the Tonga Islands arrive in Polynesia?

Incised motifs and red slips

Bits of Lapita pottery have been found scattered in archaeological digs around the Pacific. The fragments of earthenware pottery (called sherds) found in archaeological digs indicate that some of the original pots were highly decorated

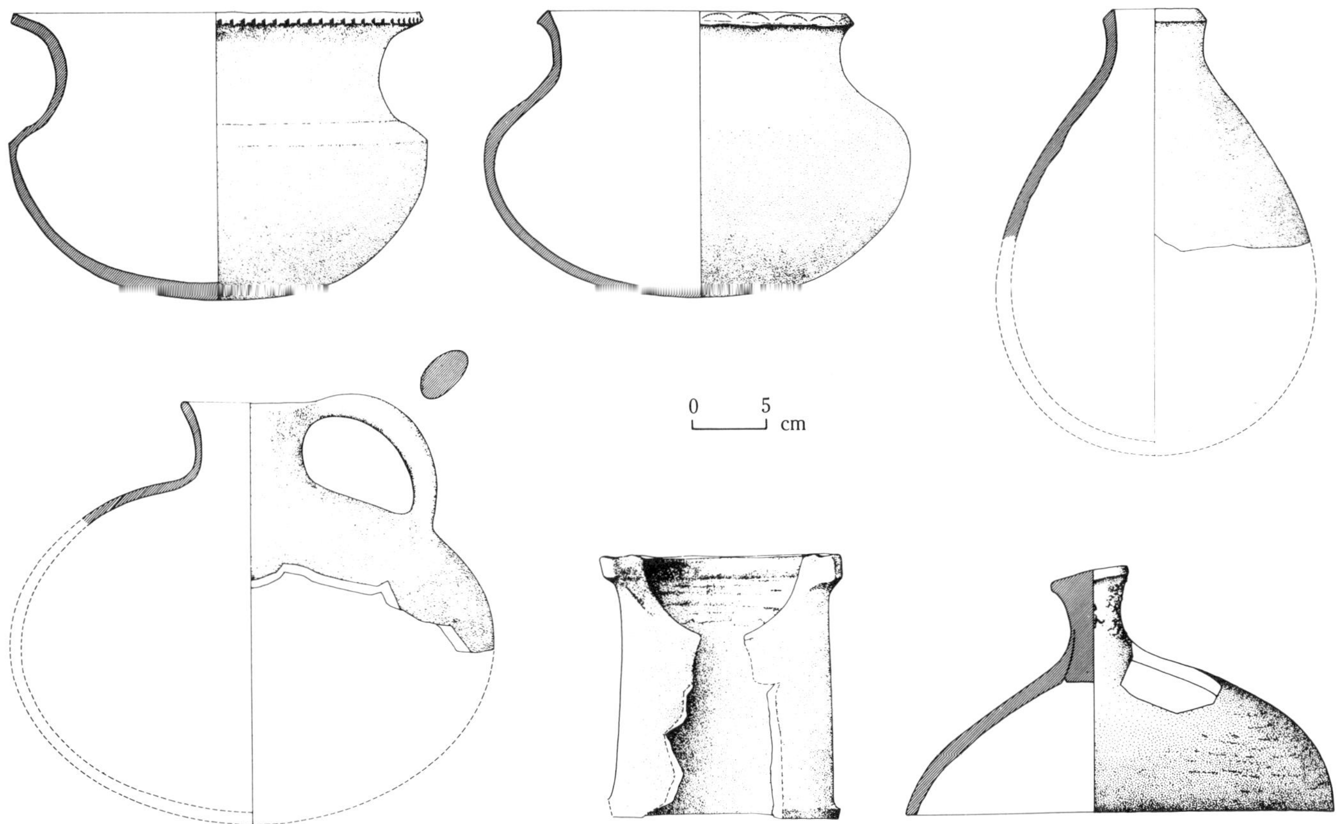

Fig. 3. Lapita designs.

with closely spaced, finely incised and repetitive motifs. Using a hand tool made from teeth, these patterns were stamped on a wide variety of pots, mixing bowls, storage jars, and cooking utensils. Wooden paddles, fingernails and shells were also used to incise or stamp the distinctive patterns. A red clay solution, or slip, was often applied to the finished pot. The majority of pots, perhaps ninety per cent, were not decorated. Several stages of development have been noticed by archaeologists. A decorative style known as Incised or Decorated Lapita pottery seems to have been followed by a plain style now known as Lapita Plainware pottery.

Obsidian, a dark-coloured volcanic rock or lava (often called bottle glass) is usually found with the Lapita pottery sherds. Obsidian was used in the making of the pots and its source has been traced to the Talasea Peninsula on New Britain and Lou Island in the nearby Manus group of islands.

In the last twenty years, archaeologists have found Lapita pottery sherds and obsidian as far afield as the Marquesas in the eastern Pacific, and Ponphei (Ponape) in the north Pacific. These have been traced along trade networks back to pottery makers in the Bismarck Archipelago. Archaeologists therefore have described quite accurately the time, distance and direction of the spread of Lapita culture in the Pacific.

Traders, voyagers and farmers

Between 4000 BP and 1600 BP these Lapita pottery makers were not only skilled potters. Archaeological digs on Eloaue Island have indicated they lived in quite large villages and relied not only on the sea but on the land for gardening and animal husbandry. They were skilled navigators and sailors, transporting obsidian from Lou and Talasea to the clay sources on Eloaue Island. This was a 450 kilometre direct voyage across open sea. From Baloff Cave on the island of New Ireland (another Lapita dig) it was a 600 kilometre voyage to obtain obsidian from Talasea.

Baloff shelter, New Ireland

Several years ago archaeologists and historians started giving the word 'Lapita' a new meaning. It became associated not only with a style of pottery, but with a particular way of life. Called Lapita culture, this lifestyle was first known by the following characteristics: skilled sea-faring; fishing; small, nomadic settlement; and long-distance trading.

The digs at the Baloff cave, on New Britain, and at Eloaue Island, have shown some other interesting features of these people. The Baloff cave or shelter is one of the major archaeological discoveries affecting knowledge of Lapita culture (see Fig. 5).

Fig. 4. Locate this region on a larger Pacific map. At a canoe speed of 6 kilometres per hour, how long would it take for a return Eloaue-Talasea voyage?

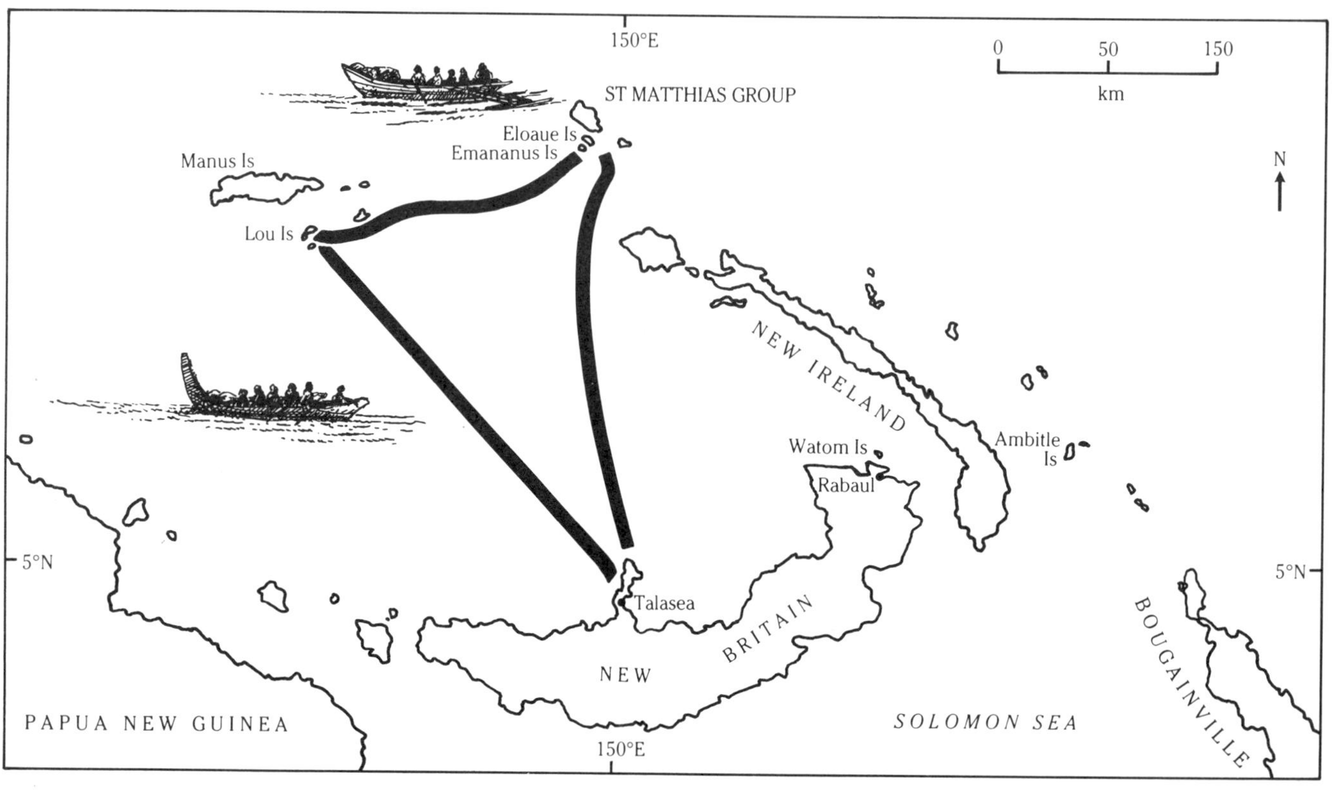

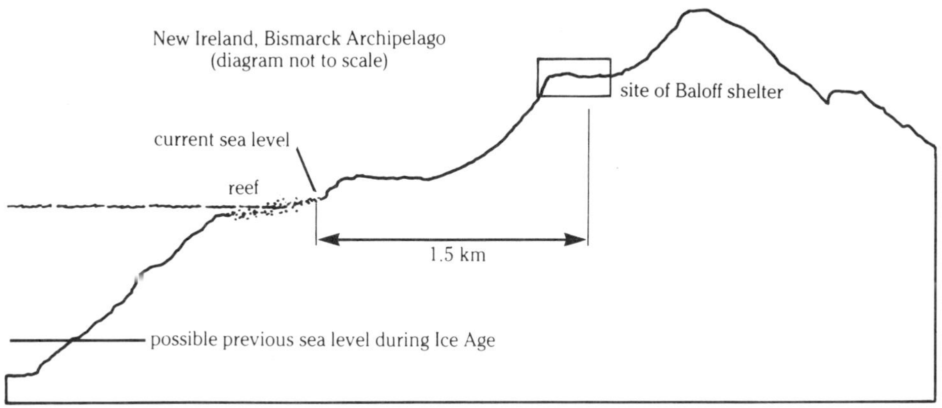

Fig. 5. The Baloff Shelter on New Ireland.

The site, about 1.5 kilometres inland from the coast of New Ireland, was first examined in 1969. It has eight levels of deposits showing extensive signs of human occupation for at least the last 7000 years. The evidence found on each level indicates the changes in lifestyle which occurred at successive stages of occupation. This evidence suggests several possible characteristics:

- ▲ a wide-ranging trade network
- ▲ significant changes in diet over the centuries
- ▲ possible changes in economic organisation (from hunting and gathering to pig farming)
- ▲ a culture based on large, permanent settlements (compared to previous ideas that Lapita culture was a small and mostly nomadic culture)
- ▲ settlements well away from the sea-shore (even further than 1.5 kilometres from the shore when Ice Age sea-levels were lower than they are today, see Figs 5 and 6).

Hundreds of Lapita sites have now been identified in the north, eastern, central and south-west Pacific, and on the coasts and off-shore islands of Papua New Guinea.

These sites were once prehistoric villages or settlements where Lapita pottery was used. The digs have uncovered layers of artefacts — pig bones, shell fish, charcoal, seeds, fish bones, and broken bits of earthenware pottery — which can be given a year date accurately by a laboratory-testing method known as radio-carbon dating.

The problem of getting a date

There are several intriguing questions about the original Lapita potters.

- ▲ Was it a skill brought from Asia or South-east Asia and carried to Melanesia when sea-levels were much lower?
- ▲ Was it a development unique to western or eastern Melanesia?

After Lapita culture was established in Melanesia, it is generally accepted that through long sea voyages for trading and settlement, Lapita potters took their pots further out into the Pacific. They voyaged, traded and settled as far east as the Marquesas and as far north as the Caroline Islands. Three further questions remain:

▲ When was Lapita culture carried into Polynesia?
▲ Were other people already occupying parts of Polynesia?
▲ Why did the use of Lapita pottery disappear?

Archaeologists have shown quite clearly that by 1600 BP the use of Lapita pottery had died out, not only in Polynesia but also in Melanesia.

In Polynesia a different lifestyle developed without pottery. This could have been because they lacked the right clay and minerals for firing pots or perhaps they had plentiful daily supplies of natural land and marine food supplies. They may have discovered the half-coconut shell as a container. In Melanesia a new culture or lifestyle also developed without the use of Lapita pottery. It is still not known why this pottery-making lifestyle disappeared.

ACTIVITIES

1 Match an event or suggested event from the text with each of the following dates: 40 000 BP; 33 000 BP; 18 000 BP; 11 000 BP; 9000 BP; 4000 BP; 1600 BP.

2 Write answers to these questions.

- **a** What is the currently accepted date for the arrival of the first Polynesians in Tonga?
- **b** Name four island groups in Polynesia.
- **c** When did Lapita culture disappear?
- **d** List four methods used to incise patterns on Lapita pottery.
- **e** What are the two main styles of Lapita pottery?
- **f** Where were the pottery maker's two main sources of obsidian?
- **g** What is a sherd?
- **h** What dates are given for the oldest artefacts found in the Baloff shelter?
- **i** Why didn't Polynesians continue with pottery making?

New evidence: sea-level changes

In 1986 two archaeologists, John Gibbons and Fergus Clunie, suggested that changes in the sea-level due to the Ice Ages provided crucial evidence that had been overlooked in earlier theories on Lapita culture and Polynesian origins.

They argued that between 18 000 and 4000 BP the sea level gradually rose and that around 18 000 BP the sea shore was 50 metres lower than it is now, and could have been as much as 120 metres lower. It gradually rose to approximately its current level about 4000 years ago. (This date coincides with the earliest known artefacts of Lapita culture, but a connection between the two has yet to be proved.)

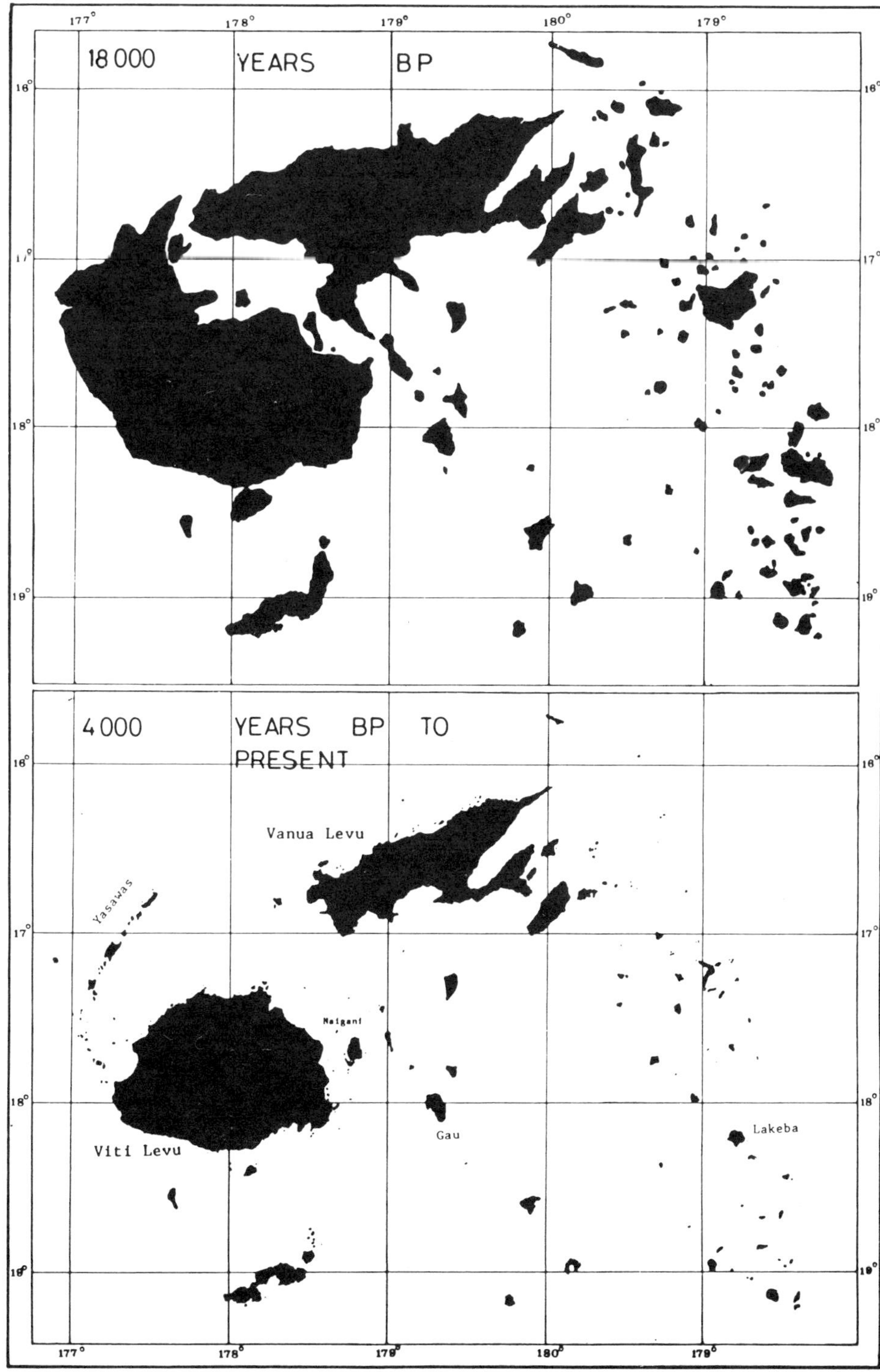

Fig. 6. *Appearance of Fiji coastline 18 000 BP and 4000 BP to present. Does a rising sea-level limit or enhance chances for survival? Is a loss of land compensated by increased shorelines used for fishing and other sea foods? Does a rising sea level cause people to leave an island or merely shift to previously vacant and 'new' coastline?*

Gibbons and Clunie noted that the land itself may have risen but only fractionally. For example, the accepted rate is a 1 metre rise in the land every 1000 years. At the same time, if Gibbons and Clunie are correct, the sea was rising perhaps 8.5 metres each 1000 years.

Based on this information, they put forward the theory that the populations then occupying South-East Asia and Melanesia had to compete for less and less land as the sea rose. Some cultures disappeared altogether when they were conquered, and some moved inland into highland areas. Gibbons and Clunie suggested that some may have migrated elsewhere in search of a home — perhaps becoming the original Polynesians. This move could have taken place at an earlier date, well before the presently accepted 4000 BP — possibly as early as 9000 BP. They pointed out that in 9000 BP, when sea-levels were lower, the land mass of each island would have been much larger and voyages between islands much shorter. It would therefore have been much easier to cross the distances now covered by open seas.

The two archaeologists argued that this theory had not been previously put forward, because the rising sea-levels after 9000 BP had covered possible signs of earlier occupation. In 1986, after diving expeditions they felt they had enough evidence to offer a new theory on Polynesian origins. This evidence included:

- ▲ the discovery of cave sites 40–80 metres underwater in Tuvalu and Tonga
- ▲ more accurate measuring of sea-level changes in the period since 18 000 BP (the last Ice Age)
- ▲ new research on blood types and languages in Polynesia, suggesting a much longer period of mixing and development than could have occurred since 4000 BP.

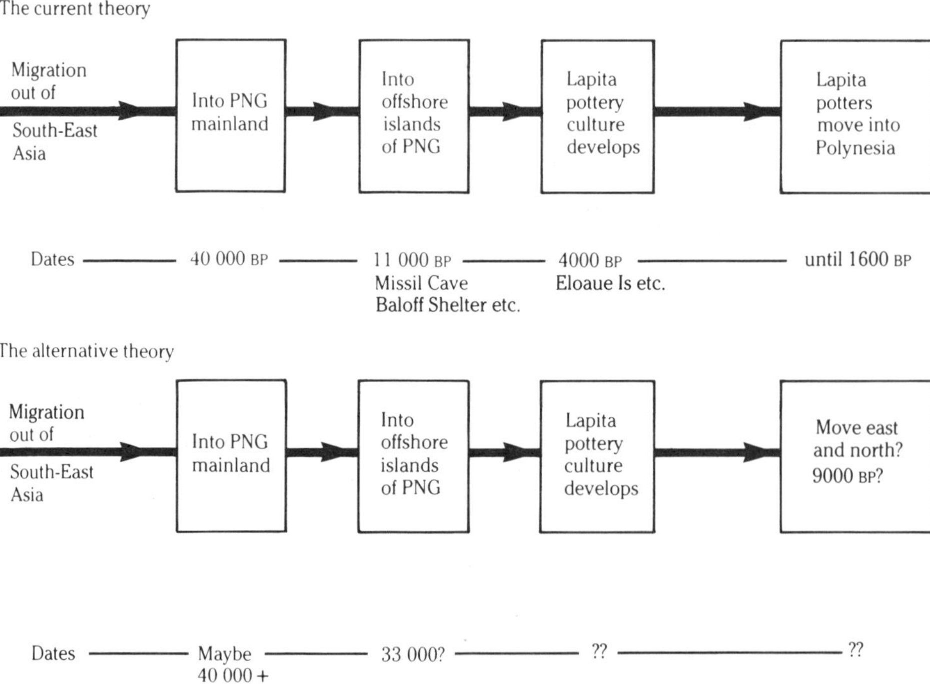

Fig. 7. Migrations: first settlers and Polynesia. If leaving a land-based culture what might have been the logical pathway across the Pacific used by the original settlers to get to Polynesia? If the original settlers were a sea-going maritime culture what other options were there for a pathway to Polynesia?

The failure of other digs in the Pacific to uncover any signs of Lapita culture before 4000 BP further supported their claims. If this new theory was accepted then it meant a radical alteration of some 5000 years to the date of arrival of the first Polynesians.

Unacceptable . . . but interesting!

In 1987, Peter Bellwood, a well known and respected expert on Polynesian prehistory, replied to Gibbons and Clunie. Bellwood disagreed with their theory. He pointed out that as the sea-level rose the original sea-faring and marine cultures of South-east Asia and Melanesia would in fact have had more sea-shore to live beside. Rising seas would have created more bays, islands and gulfs. Bellwood also claimed it was unlikely that overcrowding would have occurred as these early culture groups had low populations. Competition would have been unlikely, noted Bellwood, as numbers were small and they lived in well spread-out fishing, hunting and gathering communities.

Bellwood rejected the blood type and language arguments because he was suspicious of the investigations and research upon which these claims were made. Bellwood suggested that the best clues could be found in agricultural techniques, changing economic organisation and changing environments. But he did agree that it was possible there might be an earlier settlement date for Polynesia.

While Bellwood did not accept this new theory, he pointed out that he had been stimulated by Gibbons and Clunie's attempt to provide a new interpretation of the past. Bellwood concluded by saying 'I think we must all keep our minds open for the receipt of new data and new viewpoints'.

Another cave . . . another theory

In March 1988, it was announced that a group of archaeologists had discovered a cave at Matenkupkum. The shells and flaked stone tools seemed to indicate human occupation on the off-shore islands of Papua New Guinea around 33 000 years ago. This is an amazing 22 000 years earlier than everyone previously agreed upon! It will be some time before archaeologists sift through their findings and develop an accurate picture of what the site means.

(It is worth noting that at the time this book was being printed, archaeological digs were being carried out in dozens of sites across the Pacific in an attempt to answer unresolved questions about the prehistoric settlement of the Pacific.)

ACTIVITIES

1 Complete your map (see p. 4), by using symbols for items of trade and arrows to show direction of migration. Title your map 'Prehistoric Trade and Migration in the Bismarck Archipelago'.

2 Using arrows or lines with different colours to represent the different theories, illustrate the major directions and dates of migrations in and out of this area.

3 Check your first statement on archaeologists and rewrite it by adding or deleting five or six words.

4 Using this new sentence, make a paragraph by adding two more sentences describing the work of archaeologists in relation to Lapita culture.

5 Write answers to these questions.
- **a** Why do you think Lapita culture groups would want to migrate from Melanesia to islands in Polynesia?
- **b** How do you think Lapita pottery got from the Bismarck Archipelago to the Marquesas Islands some 5000 kilometres to the east?
- **c** If there were people in Polynesia before Lapita culture arrived, what happened to them when the new traders and settlers came?
- **d** Why do you think Lapita culture disappeared?

RESEARCH PROJECTS

1 Read Thor Heyerdahl's controversial book, *The Kon-Tiki Expedition*.

2 Make a large outline map of the Pacific, and by arrows and symbols show your own theory on Polynesian origins.

3 Research and compare the origins of the Melanesians and the Australian Aborigines.

4 Research and then describe the spread of Austronesian languages in Asia, Australia and Melanesia.

5 Check an encyclopaedia or reference book to see what they say about the origins of the Polynesians and if there is an entry for Lapita pottery.

6 Investigate the use of the words Polynesia, Micronesia and Melanesia. Where are they used and how useful are they for describing the people of the Pacific?

7 Watch the documentary 'Man on the Rim; the Peopling of the Pacific', especially part 10, or read the book, available from bookshops.

8 Find out about any recent archaeological digs. What artefacts have been found? What do they mean? What new or alternative theories are being based on this new information?

Resources

Allen, J. 'In search of the Lapita homeland: reconstructing the prehistory of the Bismarck Archipelago', *Journal of Pacific History*, vol 19, no. 3–4, 1984.

'Archaeologists uncover ancient history in Truk and Saipan', *Pacific Islands Monthly*, June 1978.

Bafmatuk, F., Egloff B. & Kaiku R. 'Islanders past and present', *Hemisphere*, vol 25, no. 2, 1980.

'Fire cave points to early mariners', *Age*, Melbourne, 13 April 1987.

Green, R. C. 'Lapita', in *The Prehistory of Polynesia*, ed. J. D. Jennings, ANU Press, Canberra, 1979.

Green, R. C. 'Lapita pottery and the origins of Polynesian culture', *Australian Natural History*, vol 17, 1973.

'Stone tools reveal skilled sailors of 40 000 years ago', *Age*, Melbourne, 9 March 1988.

Spriggs, M. 'The Lapita cultural complex; origins, distribution, contemporaries and successors', *Journal of Pacific History*, vol 19, no. 3–4, 1984.

2 Young Men, Yams and Art: Abelam History and Tradition

Focus question

What is the difference between traditional and 'airport' art?

Initiations and harvest in Abelam

The 40 000 Abelam people of Papua New Guinea people live in an area between the Sepik River and the Prince Alexander Mountains, a coastal range in the north-west of Papua New Guinea. The carvings, paintings and decorated materials they produce are part of their ceremony of male initiation and part of their celebration of the annual yam harvest.

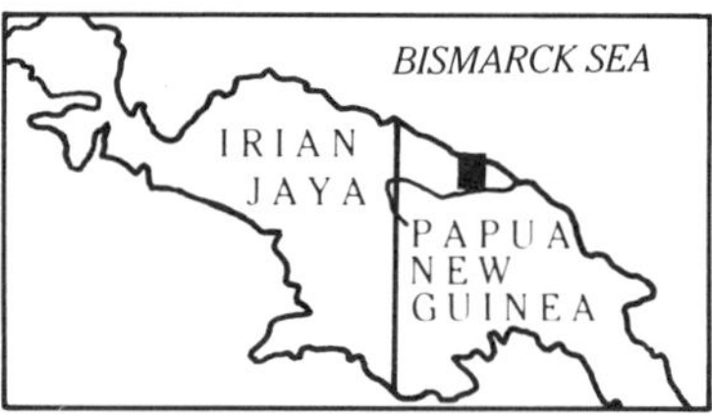

Fig. 8. Abelam, Papua New Guinea. What is the greatest distance between the Abelam villages shown on the map? Can you tell by the river patterns whether this is flat or rugged terrain? Who would the Abelam probably trade with: the Arapesh, Boiken, Chambri or Iatmul people?

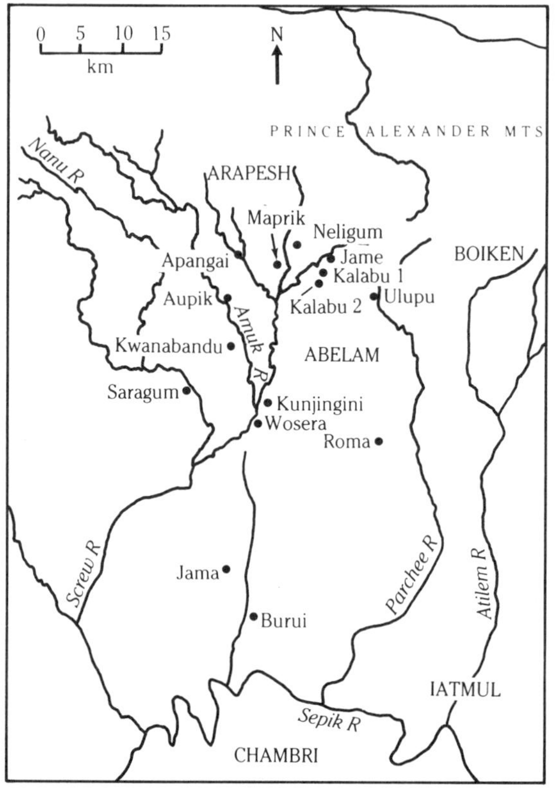

The Abelam people produce a great many carvings and paintings. Abelam is one of the most well known areas in the world for the production of indigenous or tribal art.

The message or meaning of art

Carvings, paintings and sculptures are produced in many places around the world — on canvas, paper, walls, wood, clay, metal, stone, woven material, skins, bones and glass. By looking at this art it is possible to tell something about the artists and the time in which they lived. Art can be for decoration, and it can have a message. The paintings of the artists who travelled with the explorers, James Cook and Louis Antoine Bougainville, tell us about the people of Tahiti at the time they were first seen by Europeans in the late 18th century. The wall murals or pottery decorations from ancient Crete, Mycaenae, Greece or Rome record births, deaths, battles and feasts hundreds of years before the birth of Christ. Frederick McCubbin's painting, *Down on his Luck*, reveals what Australians thought of the outback landscape or bush in the 1890s.

However, the art of European (or Western) artists is often only for decoration. Although some art works are designed to support a particular political belief or philosophy, many do not have any special meaning or purpose other than to be pleasant or interesting to look at.

Traditional and modern influences

Pacific Island art from Polynesia, Melanesia and Micronesia demonstrates many variations in the way in which form, colour, shape and size are used in art. The art of the Pacific is revealed in mats, tapa cloth, canoes, houses, human bodies, costumes, utensils and weapons, dance, drama, and song. In all cases it is an important part of the culture of the people. Vilisoni Tausie from Rotuma Island north of Fiji, describes it this way:

> The life of the Pacific people revolves around their art. Carving, dancing, music, drama, pottery, sculpture and weaving in an endless variety of ways and patterns . . . they create a sense of identity . . . creative expression, besides satisfying the creative urge in each of us, gives pleasure and personal enrichment.

Vilisoni's opinion is that art is created because there is a need for identity, for pleasure and for personal enrichment.

The art of the Pacific, in the many forms it takes, has also changed as the culture and life of the people has changed. At a particular month, year, decade or century in the past, the pottery, painting, carving or weaving was traditional because it inherited some features from a previous and older generation. But it might also have been modern because it picked up some new ideas, new techniques or new materials. For example, in Tonga in 1800 AD there were various forms of art, but they were different from the art of a thousand years before in year 800 AD. In the future there will be another version of Tongan, or modern Tongan art.

Fig. 9. Melanesian art in the Australian Museum, Sydney. Is this an anthropomorphic or zoomorphic figure?

Artists have always shown a willingness to use ideas from the past as well as new ideas. So there will always be both traditional and modern art and sometimes it will be difficult to distinguish the origins of the colours, shapes, and forms the artist is creating.

▲▲▲ Related questions ▲▲▲

1 What does art mean in the life of the Abelam people?

2 Why is Abelam art so famous?

3 Do Europeans and indigenous people look at art differently?

ACTIVITY

Select any three pieces of art such as a painting, sculpture or carving. These might include a picture from a book, a painting hanging in the Principal's office, a carving on display in the library or a famous item in a museum. Draw this table in your notebooks and fill in the descriptions. (The first one has been filled in as an example.)

Describe the piece	Name of artist	When created	Explain why you think it was created by the artist
1 Painting. Down on his Luck *has a man sitting in the bush by a small fire holding his head looking sad and defeated.*	*Frederick McCubbin*	*1889*	*I think McCubbin was trying to show that although the bush was beautiful, life in the Australian bush could be rather hard, miserable and lonely.*
2			
3			

Abelam artists

The Abelam people of north-west Papua New Guinea create several forms of art for the male initiation ceremony. This art is mostly carved wooden figures decorated with paint, brightly coloured leaves, bark and feathers. The bark of the sago palm is also painted and brightly decorated. The Abelam are also famous for the architecture and decoration of their korombo, the enormous A-frame spirit houses which soar as high as 20 metres above ground. It is used to store sacred and magic objects. It is also used for the performance of special ceremonies. In parts of the Sepik area of Papua New Guinea these houses are called Haus Tamboran or men's houses.

Describe the Abelam art figures (Figures 9 and 10) in your notebooks. Explain the relevance of each to the past culture.

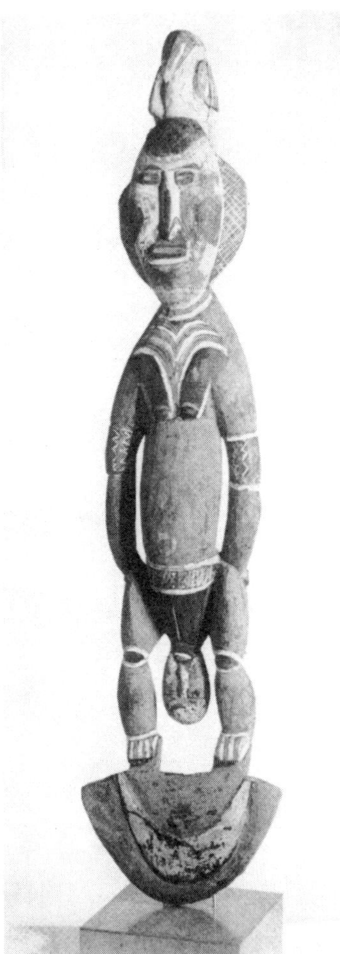

Fig. 10. List the materials which the artist used to make this figure. What human features has the artist included? Can you tell by looking at it whether it represents a living, dead or spirit person?

Context and meaning

The art of the Abelam people has a special place in their daily lives. Western or European artists present objects (carvings, paintings, sculptures) just for the sake of doing them or for the purpose of letting others look at them. Western or European artists are not as concerned about letting the viewer know why an object of art was produced.

In contrast to this, Abelam paintings and carvings are produced because they are part of their custom and culture. They have meaning. Anthropologists describe this by saying that Abelam art has a special context so that when the Abelam produce each painted and carved figure or mask, it can be linked to a particular young man's initiation into adulthood, or a particular year's yam harvest. (A yam is a large, starchy, tropical root crop, often wrongly called a sweet potato.)

Yams and chambera

The planting, gardening, harvesting and cooking of yams is of major importance in the life of the Abelam people. Men also gain prestige and become known as village leaders through growing and trading yams with partners in neighbouring villages or with other men in their own village. These yam trading partners are called chambera and a competition exists between them to see which partner can arrange the best initiation ceremony or produce the best yams. When the artist creates a carving or painting it is therefore part of the chambera, and at the same time a part of a young man's initiation ceremony.

The artists of Abelam produce two types of figures. Some are like humans (called anthropomorphic figures) and some are like animals (called zoomorphic figures.) The preparation of the carvings for the initiation ceremony takes nine months.

As you read on, construct a timeline of events concerned with the initiation and the creation of the art for the ceremony. The dates for some events in this sequence have already been mentioned. List each date and event in the correct order.

'If the idea comes from inside the man'

Usually in September, during the rainy season before the yam harvest, men go into the forest to select hardwood trees and begin to carve their figures. The men stay away in the forest for a few days at a time and work at their individual carvings in groups of two or three. Although they cooperate and work together there is no copying. Each carving is the creation of the individual who worked on it. An anthropologist, Diane Losche, who lived with the Abelam in 1976 and 1977, asked one Abelam carver what this meant. He replied that 'a man cannot imitate or try to copy a carving exactly. His carving will only be good if the idea comes from inside the man himself'. In April or May, just after the yam harvest, the men of the village meet to decide if the harvest has been good enough to celebrate, and therefore that an initiation can take place.

The initiation ceremony

If they agree that the yam harvest has been successful, the Korombo is fenced and, for up to a month, the artists and the young men to be initiated are separated from the rest of the village.

Nine months pass from the time the artists first select trees in the forest for the carvings. During the final preparation young men who have already been initiated gather leaves and feathers from the forest. The older men who are conducting the initiation begin to finely carve, paint and decorate the carefully selected wooden and bark figures.

All the carvings and bark paintings prepared for the initiation ceremony are secretly brought to the spirit house and given their final bright decorations. The Abelam build these giant spirit houses around the amei or cleared village square. Magic acts are performed in the dark to prepare the spirit house for the initiation and each carving or painting is given the name (or nggwal) of an ancestor.

The initiation ceremony involves the young men being carried quickly through the darkened spirit house. They undergo some form of physical pain before returning to view and be told the meaning of the secret, magic and sacred objects, carvings and paintings inside the Korombo. All this takes place inside a fenced area which is taboo for all women and other villagers and neighbours.

After the initiation ceremony a dance is held. The young initiated men are allowed to move out into the village. Women also attend the dance. The 'new' men decorate and dress themselves to look like the painted carvings. They take the name of the nggwal the paintings represent.

At the end of the ceremony the paintings and carvings are destroyed, or perhaps saved for a future but less important ceremony. They have served their purpose. The yams have been harvested and a new group of young men have been initiated. For the next harvest or the next initiation, Abelam artists will create another set of paintings and carvings.

The dance held after the initiation ceremony marks the end of the creative period. The young men who have been initiated, and the older men who have taken them through the ceremony and created the carvings and paintings, dress themselves for the dance. They become as elaborate and brightly decorated as the art they have created. The artists and young men display themselves in the village so that the women of their community can admire and perhaps be attracted to them.

ACTIVITY

Write answers to these questions.

a What are the two types of figures which Abelam artists create?

b What do these Abelam words mean in English?

- ▲ amei
- ▲ korombo
- ▲ chambera
- ▲ nggwal

c How long before the initiation ceremony does selection of suitable timber occur?

d What is the criterion for deciding whether an initiation ceremony will be held?

e During the final preparations of the figures and paintings what do

- ▲ the younger men do?
- ▲ the older men do?

f What event is held to mark the end of the initiation ceremony?

g What happens to the carved figures when the ceremony is over?

In museums and galleries

In museums and art galleries all around the world the art of the Abelam people can be observed. These objects were obtained, often disrespectfully and even illegally many years ago by government officials, explorers, missionaries, researchers, art dealers and casual visitors.

As these objects of art sit or hang on display in New York, Paris or Melbourne, they allow visitors to the gallery to observe an indigenous and unique culture and tradition. But how many gallery visitors really understand what these objects mean to the Abelam people?

Airport art

In the twentieth century the artists of the Pacific are under great pressure. More and more visitors, museums, galleries and private collectors want examples of 'primitive' or 'traditional native' art. What will happen if the art is taken away from the people who created it? Does it still have a special meaning or does it become merely a decoration to be looked at with interest or curiosity by people on the other side of the world?

Linked to this are three important changes. One is the move of many villagers to the cities or tourist resort areas; the second is the adoption by many Islanders of more 'modern' or 'western' ways of life; the third is the adoption by many Islanders of a Christian religion which often does not accept that their art has a magical, spirit relationship with ancestors.

Because of these changes art may not have the same meaning for these groups of people once they have moved and adopted new ideas and ways. Does this mean that the artist's skills and the meaning of the art will disappear? Will the art which links them to the past and their very own culture disappear as well?

More and more tourists are also visiting the Pacific and they like to take home souvenirs. Pacific Islanders are also keen to earn money to buy manufactured goods, to pay their taxes, to repay debts, or to give away in special ceremonies or rituals. The result is that it is now possible to buy carvings (and other art forms) at airports, shipping terminals and roadside markets or stalls wherever you travel in the Pacific. Why was this art created? Is it the spiritual and meaningful art of the people?

One advantage of the increase in 'airport art', as these cheap and mass produced carvings are called, is that it has sparked a new interest in old styles of carving and traditional or custom art in general. It has led some people in the islands to search back and to follow the traditions of their ancestors. Many communities now include traditional or custom art as part of the school curriculum or offer it as a community arts and crafts program. The impact of these changes is still not clear. What will the art of the Pacific be like in the future?

ACTIVITIES

1 Write answers to these questions.

- **a** What do you think are the main differences between Abelam artists and western or European artists?
- **b** Why do you think the yam is so important to Abelam people?
- **c** Why do you think the giving of the nggwal names of ancestors and spirits is so important?
- **d** Why do you think young boys are initiated?
- **e** Why do you think the initiation ceremony is kept secret from women in the village?

f The details about the Abelam in this chapter were gathered in 1976 and 1977. How long do you think these people will continue like this, practising and believing in their traditional culture and traditions? What might cause them to change?
g What is the difference between modern art and traditional art?
h In one sentence explain the meaning of the phrase 'traditional art'.

2 Look back to your table where you described three pieces of art (see page 16). Would you change your comments in the fourth column?

3 Choose one illustration used in this unit and list five questions you would need to ask the artist in order to find out why it was created? For example: How old were you when this was made?

RESEARCH PROJECT

1 Visit a gallery which has exhibits of Pacific art. Check to see how adequately the items are described. Do the tags try and place the item in the context of the culture from which it came? Do they say what it is? Do they explain its meaning?

2 Research some of the other forms of art in the Pacific such as
- ▲ Lapita pottery decoration
- ▲ body decoration and tattooing
- ▲ headdresses
- ▲ masks
- ▲ shield making and decoration of weapons
- ▲ canoe prows and decorations

3 Select one Pacific Island culture group, for example, French Polynesians (from Tahiti), Easter Islanders, or Fijians, and research their art forms.

4 If you get the opportunity visit the Australian Museum in Sydney. It has a permanent award-winning exhibition on the art, culture and lifestyle of the Abelam people.

Resources

Barrow, T. *The Art of Tahiti*, Thames and Hudson, London, 1979.
Ebin, V. *The Body Decorated*, Thames and Hudson, London, 1980.
Feest, C. *The Art of War*, Thames and Hudson, London, 1980.
Losche, D. 'Abelam history', *Hemisphere*, vol 25, no. 2, 1980.
Tausie, V. *Art in the New Pacific*, USP/Institute for Pacific Studies, Suva, 1980.

3 Living in a Volcano: A Violent History

Focus question

What impact do natural disasters have on Pacific Island people?

Fig. 11. Rabaul Harbour. The low-lying coastal area would be the first hit by gas, lava, ash and wave action. Would the ridges behind be any safer?

The Rabaul caldera

One kilometre underground, below the city of Rabaul on the island of New Britain in Papua New Guinea, there is a vast cave or magma chamber full of fluid rock and gas. This hot fluid rock and gas will surge the one kilometre to the surface, erupt and cover Rabaul with ash, molten lava, smoke and flying fiery particles, perhaps within the next few years.

Rabaul is a city surrounded by smaller active volcanoes but, more significantly, below it is a vast unpredictable chamber of volcanic material.

Volcanic activity is common in Papua New Guinea. In January 1951 in the eastern highlands of Papua New Guinea, the Orokaiva people knew that something strange was happening. On January 20 a column of vapour and ash extended 8000 metres in the air above nearby Mt Lamington. The next day, as many Orokaiva people were preparing to go home from Sunday church services or were talking or resting in their houses, earth tremors and huge explosions caused the earth to shake. The sky was black for two hours. An enormous blast was heard 150 kilometres away in Port Moresby on the other side of the central mountain range. It was also heard in Lae, 300 kilometres to the north. Over 177 square kilometres of housing and vegetation was totally destroyed. More than 4000 people were killed. A new episode had been added to the legends which had been passed down by the Orokaiva people each generation since Mt Lamington had erupted a thousand years before.

The Orokaiva people had seen signs for more than a week that something strange was happening to the mountain. In Rabaul on the Gazelle Peninsula, everyone knows that they are also sitting on a volcano. What they would like to know is when the magma will finally burst through the earth's surface and release all its destructive energy. How long will it be before this bottled-up energy creates the next eruption in the Pacific Islands' long history of volcanic activity?

When researching the history of the Pacific Islands, historians look for patterns. If an event is repeated over the period of a decade, a century or perhaps

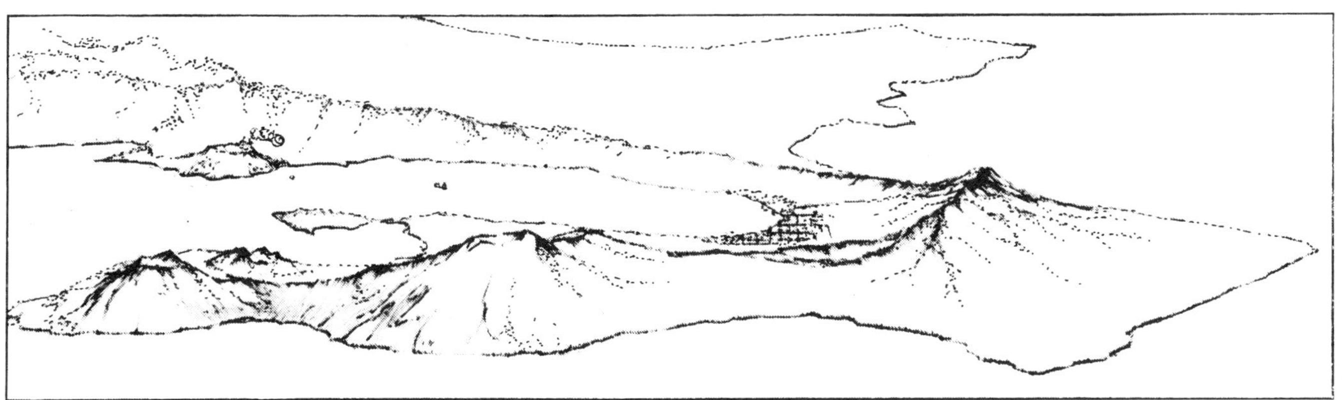

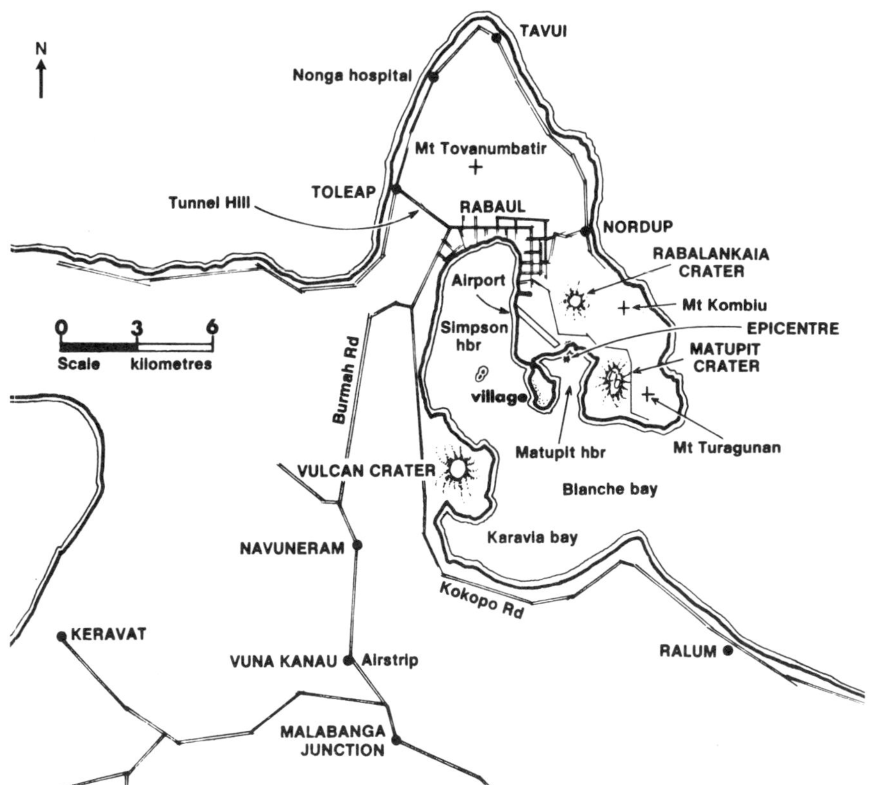

BELOW: A caldera. Expulsion of lava (A) from the magma chamber (B) may leave the central core (C) without support. A collapse results in a large, steep-sided caldera (D). The magma chamber may cool and solidify (E), allowing water to collect in the caldera (F).

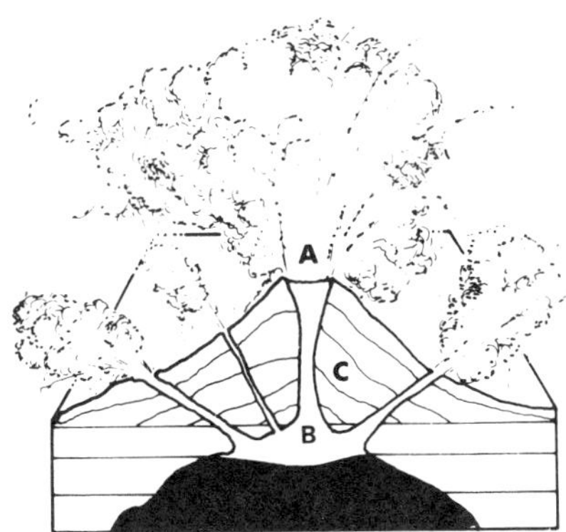

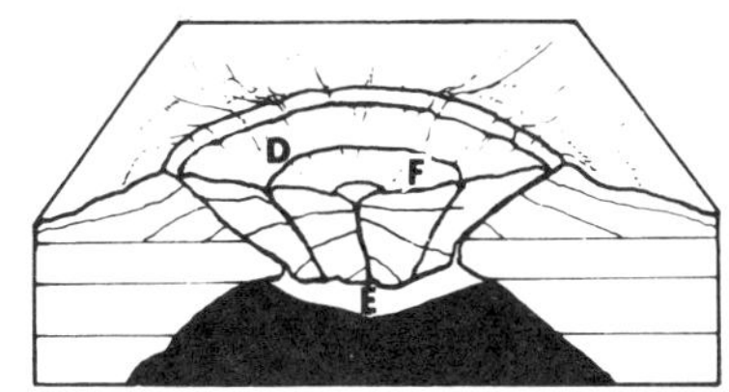

Fig. 12. The rim of a volcanic caldera; a map of Rabaul and its harbour; a caldera. Where is the rim of the ancient caldera? How many volcanic cones and craters surround Rabaul? If a Stage 4 Alert (see p. 26) and evacuation was called where would the greatest congestion be?

thousands of years, or if similar events have occurred in more than one place, then the event is called a theme. There is no doubt that volcanic activity, and the response to volcanic eruptions and other natural disasters such as cyclones, droughts, and tsunami (seismic sea wave), is a theme in Pacific history. There is a pattern of sudden life and death stretching back for thousands of years. Depending on the unpredictable status of the magma chamber under Rabaul, the next chapter on this theme will soon be written.

▲▲▲ Related questions ▲▲▲

1. How have Islanders reacted to volcanic eruptions in the past?
2. What planning is in place to prevent a volcanic eruption causing human tragedies?
3. Why do people continue to occupy land in areas where there is a volcanic threat?
4. Which Pacific Island nations are most at threat from volcanic activity?
5. What other natural disasters affect the lives of Island people?
6. How have these events been recorded by historians?

ACTIVITIES

1. List five possible ways that a mountain, its surrounding land, and its flora and fauna might be of special importance to a local community.
2. On a map of Papua New Guinea mark in Karkar Island, Rabaul and Mt Lamington.
3. Imagine that a volcanic eruption occurs near a major Pacific island port and city. List the ten immediate consequences of the eruption.
4. If you were responsible for deciding what to send on the first emergency relief flight to a volcanic or cyclonic disaster area, what would you send? Consider the type of damage you think might occur and plan your cargo accordingly. List twenty items you would consider important.
5. Place the list of cargo items in priority order.

Lamington, Yasour and Mauna Loa

Volcanic activity is a fact of life in the Pacific. Much of the land area was created by volcanic eruptions which left drowned craters and chains of islands. The commonly used description 'high islands' refers to the many islands formed by the peaks of extinct and still active volcanoes which are above the ocean surface.

In the north Pacific in Hawaii, the eruptions of Mauna Loa and Kilauea continue to provide vulcanologists and tourists with a close glimpse of the powerful forces which create lava flows, volcanic cones, calderas and craters. In the south-west Pacific on Tanna Island in Vanuatu the accessible volcano Mt Yasour can be scaled or watched from nearby as it spews out molten ash and rock. On Savaii Island in Western Samoa, Mt Maugaafi erupted in 1760, Mt Mat-ole-Afi in 1902 and Mt Matavanu in 1905–1911. There are many active volcanoes in the Pacific. There are nine in Tonga, one in the Loyalty Islands, seven in Vanuatu, one in Santa Cruz, three in the Solomon Islands, and nineteen in Papua New Guinea. Since ancient times over 800 eruptions of active volcanoes have been recorded in writing by historians, drawings by artists and related in stories, dances, myths and legends passed down by orators and performers.

Fig. 13. Rabaul Volcano. What technique has the photographer used to show the danger of the volcano?

Stage Two Alert

Rabaul sits in a giant caldera formed by an eruption 1400 years ago, in 567 AD. The giant caldera, called Proto Rabaul, erupted with an enormous explosion leaving behind a crater 6 kilometres wide and 12 kilometres long. The sea flooded this giant caldera and created Rabaul Harbour. The flash of heat and fire from the eruption was so bright that its reflection was seen by ancient Greeks in the sky above the Mediterranean. This was a similar size to the great volcanic eruption which occurred when the Indonesian island of Krakatoa erupted and was virtually blown away on August 27 1883. The reflection of its eruption was seen around the world.

During the Second World War there were 90 000 Japanese troops in Rabaul and, to drive them out of the fortifications, American bombers dropped thousands of tons of high explosive into the craters of Rabaul's volcanoes hoping to set off an eruption. This inhumane and irresponsible plan did not work. Forty years later, it appears that nature will inevitably take its own course.

Rabaul, which suffered its last major eruption in 1937, is now preparing for the next eruption. Chris McKee, the assistant Government vulcanologist, reported several years ago that '. . . the next eruption would come some time before the end of the century and could come within two or three years'. During

Fig. 14. Rabaul market. An eruption would instantly destroy food supplies for sale in markets and shops. More serious long-term problems would result from polluted fishing streams and bays, and the loss of gardens, fruit trees and livestock.

1983 and 1984 an eruption seemed imminent and for thirteen months the district was put on a Stage Two Alert according to international disaster planning.

STAGE 1 ALERT:	ERUPTION EXPECTED WITHIN YEARS TO MONTHS
STAGE 2 ALERT:	ERUPTION EXPECTED WITHIN MONTHS TO WEEKS
STAGE 3 ALERT:	ERUPTION EXPECTED WITHIN WEEKS TO DAYS
STAGE 4 ALERT:	ERUPTION EXPECTED WITHIN DAYS TO HOURS

Emergency procedures and a disaster plan were activated, but the six active and three extinct volcanoes which surround the city of Rabaul remained quiet.

The relief was shortlived. In May 1987 Dr Peter Lowenstein, the chief Papua New Guinea vulcanologist announced that in the underground chamber or epicentre '. . . energy is still being stored. It's important to realise that another eruption at Rabaul is inevitable. We've simply been given a respite'.

Records which have been kept over the past 300 years suggest that Rabaul can expect two eruptions each hundred years. The last two were in 1878 and in 1937 when Matupit (or Tavurvur) erupted and the small island of Vulcan also dramatically appeared and became a 300 metre wide volcanic cone.

The reminders of Rabaul's violent past are easily visible. The black sand beaches, the streaks of sulphur, the smoking crater of Matupit, the towering cones of the 'Mother and Sisters' and the regular tremors indicate that living in Rabaul does indeed mean living in a volcano. Despite this, 95 000 people live in the city and surrounding district and have not yet shown any signs they will abandon Rabaul for safer ground.

Fig. 15. Matupit Island. Note the 90 m wide black sand beach which has resulted because of pressure from the subterranean magma body which is lifting the island from the sea.

Unmistakable signs

There has been no shortage of earthquakes, rumblings and tremors in Rabaul. Signs that the magma chamber is expanding or seeking an escape to the earth's surface have occurred regularly. Recent volcanic activity includes:

1973–83	Rabaul airport tarmac rises 1 metre
1976–84	Island of Matupit rises 1 metre exposing a 90 metre wide black sand beach
1983	Earthquake measuring 7.8 on March 18
1984	Earthquake measuring 7.4 on February 8
Oct 1983–Feb 1984	Seismic recorders show twenty times more underground volcanic activity

It will be a big one!

Vulcanologists believe that the magma chamber is at least as big as that which created the 1937 Rabaul eruptions. But it may be as big as the Krakatoa eruption, which was forty-five times more powerful than the Rabaul eruption of 1937. Based on observations since 1950, when the first vulcanological observatory was established, they predict that if all the magma were expelled at once rather than seeping out in a series of flows and minor explosions, the result could be equal to the Mt St Helens (USA) eruption of May 18 1980. That is, equal to the total force of 500 times the atomic bomb dropped on Hiroshima in 1945.

Dr Russell Blong, a geomorphologist, believes that the recent 5 cm lifting of the base of Matupit indicates that an enormous mass of molten lava is forcing its way to the surface. He declared in 1984 that 'it is impossible to say how big the eruption will be, but we can be sure that it will be a big one'.

The 1937 Rabaul eruption claimed 500 lives. There were no vulcanologists in Rabaul then and no disaster plan. Although there had been warnings no one took much notice. Mr Robert Winterbotham, who was aged nineteen at the time, recalled:

> We were having lunch when a native ran into the house and said 'Masta the water boils . . .' Earthquakes were very common, sometimes one or two a week — only light earthquakes, 2.4 at the most . . . the natives from the local village rushed out in their canoes picking up the dead fish . . . about 2.00 p.m. there was a terrific explosion. Two more followed. The natives in the canoes went up with it and then the villages on the coast, about two or three of them. Just wiped out . . .

Mrs Trevitt, a newcomer to the Territory of New Guinea, as it was called then, had been married that afternoon in Rabaul. She recalled:

> The smoke and sulphur fumes and falling mud and stones were blinding. The thick cloud of smoke was impenetrable . . . native people, panic stricken, were fleeing in hundreds down from the hills not knowing where to go.

That was 4.15 p.m. on Saturday 29 May 1937. Within hours, 180 people were dead. The next day Matupit erupted. Four days later Vulcan on the other side of the harbour had created a cone 300 metres high and the death toll had reached 500. Most had died of asphyxia from the dense cloud of ash and silica. Ash from the blast fell more than 240 kilometres away.

When Rabaul erupts again the level of emergency services, evacuation plans, and forewarning should prevent a major loss of lives. However, the dangers are many. The initial searing, hot blast from a big explosion could kill people caught close to the epicentre. Asphyxia would be the next danger, though 50 000 surgical masks now stored in Rabaul will provide some protection from poisonous gases and dirt-laden air. A tsunami possibly up to 60 metres high and travelling at 650 kilometres per hour, could cause destruction over a wide area, not counting the damage in the enclosed harbour where the city of Rabaul is built.

There would be the major problem of tephra or volcanic ash which could bury everything several metres, causing roofs to crash and people to be buried alive. The panic during the pitch-black darkness caused by the falling ash would create more accidents and loss of human life. The financial cost in terms of the loss in property, buildings, equipment, crops, livestock, public services and water supplies would be enormous. Furthermore, the only emergency airstrip cannot take the large cargo planes essential for evacuation and relief work. Power would also be cut because the diesel power station which supplies Rabaul's electricity is on the water's edge. A new hydro-electric scheme is clear of the possible epicentre, but power lines and relay stations close to Rabaul would certainly be destroyed.

There are eleven seismic stations monitoring activity at the six active and three extinct craters around Rabaul, as well as the four submarine vents on the nearby ocean floor. When the signs inevitably come their warning will lead to the evacuation of Rabaul — and a very big bang!

ACTIVITIES

1 Write answers to these questions.

- **a** How far underground is the magma chamber?
- **b** What does inevitable mean?
- **c** If you visited Rabaul today, what would be five visible signs that it was a volcanic area? List the five.
- **d** How many years separate the last two Rabaul eruptions?
- **e** How many years is it since the last Rabaul eruption?
- **f** For how many years have vulcanologists been at Rabaul monitoring seismic activity?

2 Using Fig. 12, explain how the harbour at Rabaul was formed. Use diagrams to help illustrate your explanation.

3 What is a caldera? Sketch a caldera and then describe it in less than twenty words.

4 In the 1937 eruption 0.4 cubic kilometres of volcanic matter erupted from Vulcan and Matupit. If the Krakatoa eruption was forty-five times bigger, how many cubic kilometres of matter did it release?

5 What impact would volcanic activity or the possibility of it have on tourism and development in the city? (See Fig. 12).

There were many heroes

In a report on the Mt Lamington disaster in Papua New Guinea one journalist wrote that there were many heroes. Three people were mentioned in the report. They were two European clergymen and a European businessman.

In the published descriptions of the Mt Lamington eruption, the most common fact presented is that thirty-six Europeans were killed. If the opinions of people are quoted, who were there before the blast or during the clean-up, they are always Europeans. The news magazine *Pacific Islands Monthly* (1951); books such as Gavin Souter's *New Guinea: the last unknown* (1963); the radio program 'Taim Bilong Masta' (1980–1981) and James Sinclair's *Last frontiers: the explorations of Ivan Champion of Papua* (1988) repeat the same details. Only when historians rely on oral history and evidence collected from the Orokaiva people will the Pacific Islanders' role in this event become more widely known.

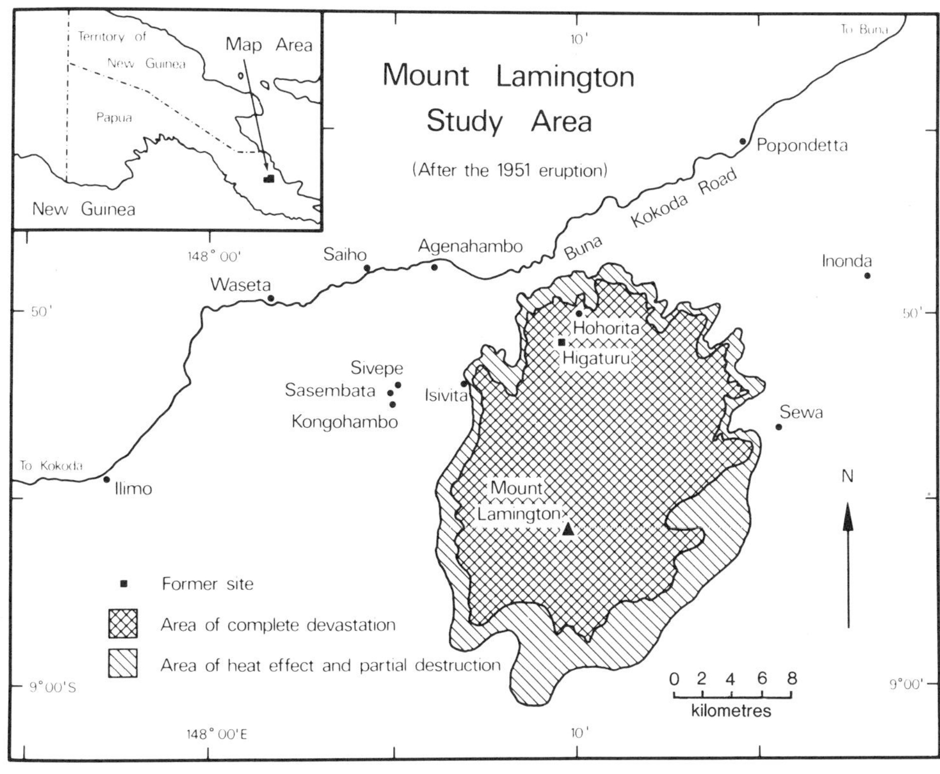

Fig. 16. Mt Lamington. Maps like this are useful for showing the physical size of the damage zone. Can you 'map' culture change, economic costs, psychological impact and spiritual impact on a flat piece of paper?

In the wake of the Mt Lamington disaster the government employed two anthropologists to report on the best policy to help people resettle the area. Several European missionaries, government officials and geologists then wrote reports on the eruption. It had become an event — a part of the written European history of Papua New Guinea.

It has also become part of the oral history of the Orokaiva and other people affected by the eruption. Fifteen years later, in 1966 and 1967, another anthropologist stayed in the area and described the local people and the social consequences and cultural shock caused by the eruption. The Orokaiva related how the mountain had been at the centre of Orokaivan religion. In their myths it was where death, warfare and fire originated. It was home to Sumbiripa, a mythical figure who died there when the mountain was first formed.

The Orokaiva believed the eruption occurred because hand grenades thrown near the mountain in the 1939–1945 war had disturbed the quietness of the mountain. Young men who had used hunting rifles nearby after the war were also blamed. Others thought that the Christian God was punishing them for not obeying the orders of the church and government quickly enough. Others thought it was a punishment for the murder of government officials who had tried to establish a coffee-growing project among the Orokaiva people.

The geological explanation for Mt Lamington was that a vent opened and a wave of hot ash came down the mountain like an avalanche. It scorched and burst the lungs of all who breathed the volcanic dust, ash and gas which had a temperature of 200 degrees. The descending cloud travelled at about 120 kilometres per hour, quickly covering the surrounding countryside for kilometres in all directions. Many were scalded badly, often fatally, by the boiling water, mud and ash which flowed down rivers for weeks afterwards.

One day soon the Rabaul caldera will also erupt. Other Pacific Islanders live amid and survive regular and equally destructive forces. They may not live on a volcano like the Rabaul and Orokaiva people, but their lifestyles may be changed by similar natural disasters. Land, good fruit-bearing trees, ancestral burial grounds and houses often disappear forever. Disputes break out because of lands created when earthquakes or eruptions create new islands and coastal plains, or when rivers change course, or good soils become infertile. Resettlement in new and distant places is often necessary because the land becomes unproductive. Aspects of traditional religions are challenged by new ideas and actions and ancient myths must be reshaped and events given new meanings.

Disasters not only reshape the land, but also the culture and lifestyle of the people. It remains to be seen what will happen if and when Rabaul erupts.

ACTIVITIES

1 Re-examine your answer to question 3 on p. 24. Add to your list of consequences. Then use numbers to rank them in order of immediate importance and concern to the local people.

2 Re-examine your answer to question 6 on p. 24. Read your list of cargo items in priority order. Change the items or change the order if you have further information which has caused you to change your mind.

3 What damage would result if a blast similar to the 1951 eruption at Mt Lamington occurred near your school? On a map of your own area, draw a square with your school approximately in the centre. The square should equal the 177 square kilometres covered by the Mt Lamington blast.

4 In one hundred years' time what aspects of the Mt Lamington eruption do you think the Orokaiva people will be including in their stories and legends?

5 Why do you think Mt Lamington erupted? Did it have anything to do with the war?

6 Rabaul has already experienced a Stage Two Alert. What precautions would be enforced if the final Stage Four Alert was declared?

7 Why do you think the 95 000 people are willing to stay in Rabaul despite the inevitable and possibly tragic eruption which is forecast?

8 In the predicted Rabaul eruption which do you think would cause the most loss of life:

▲ lava flows
▲ ash and smoke
▲ panic (leading to accidents)
▲ exploding gas

9 In a timeline of events which have occurred in the Pacific in the twentieth century, would you include the Rabaul eruptions (1937) or Mt Lamington (1951)? Explain why or why not in about fifty words.

RESEARCH PROJECTS

1 Research the discovery and introduction of the Richter scale. Who invented this technique?

2 Research and describe the eruptions which occurred at:

▲ Krakatoa (Indonesia)
▲ Vesuvius (Italy)
▲ Mt St Helens (USA)
▲ Mt Tarawera (This eruption in New Zealand in 1885 buried a whole Maori village.)

3 Construct a map showing the major active volcanoes in the world.

4 Check local newspapers and magazines when the next cyclone causes destruction in the Pacific region. Analyse the reports. What facts do they include? Do they provide information about both the physical and the human or cultural impact?

5 If you have access to a local historical society or library, you might be able to look up newspapers for eyewitness accounts of the 1937 Rabaul eruption, the 1951 Mt Lamington eruption, or one of the many recent major eruptions in Hawaii.

6 Visit a local volcano, extinct crater or lava plain.

Resources

Belshaw, C. 'Social consequences of the Mount Lamington eruption', *Oceania*, vol 21, 1951, pp. 241–252.

Brereton, E. *et al. A Geographers World: Book 3*, 'Mountains that breathe fire', Longman Cheshire, Melbourne, 1981.

Nelson, H. *Taim Bilong Masta*, Ch. 9, ABC Books, 1982.

Pacific Islands Monthly, vol 51, no. 8, August 1980, pp. 111–112.

Rogers, G. (ed.) *The Fire has Jumped*, USP/Institute for Pacific Studies, Suva, 1986.

Schwimmer, E. 'What did the eruption mean?' in *Exiles and Migrants in Oceania*, ed. M. Leiber, University of Hawaii Press, Honolulu.

4

The Highlands of Papua New Guinea: First Contact

Focus question

How did the people of the interior react to the arrival of the first white men in the Papua New Guinea Highlands?

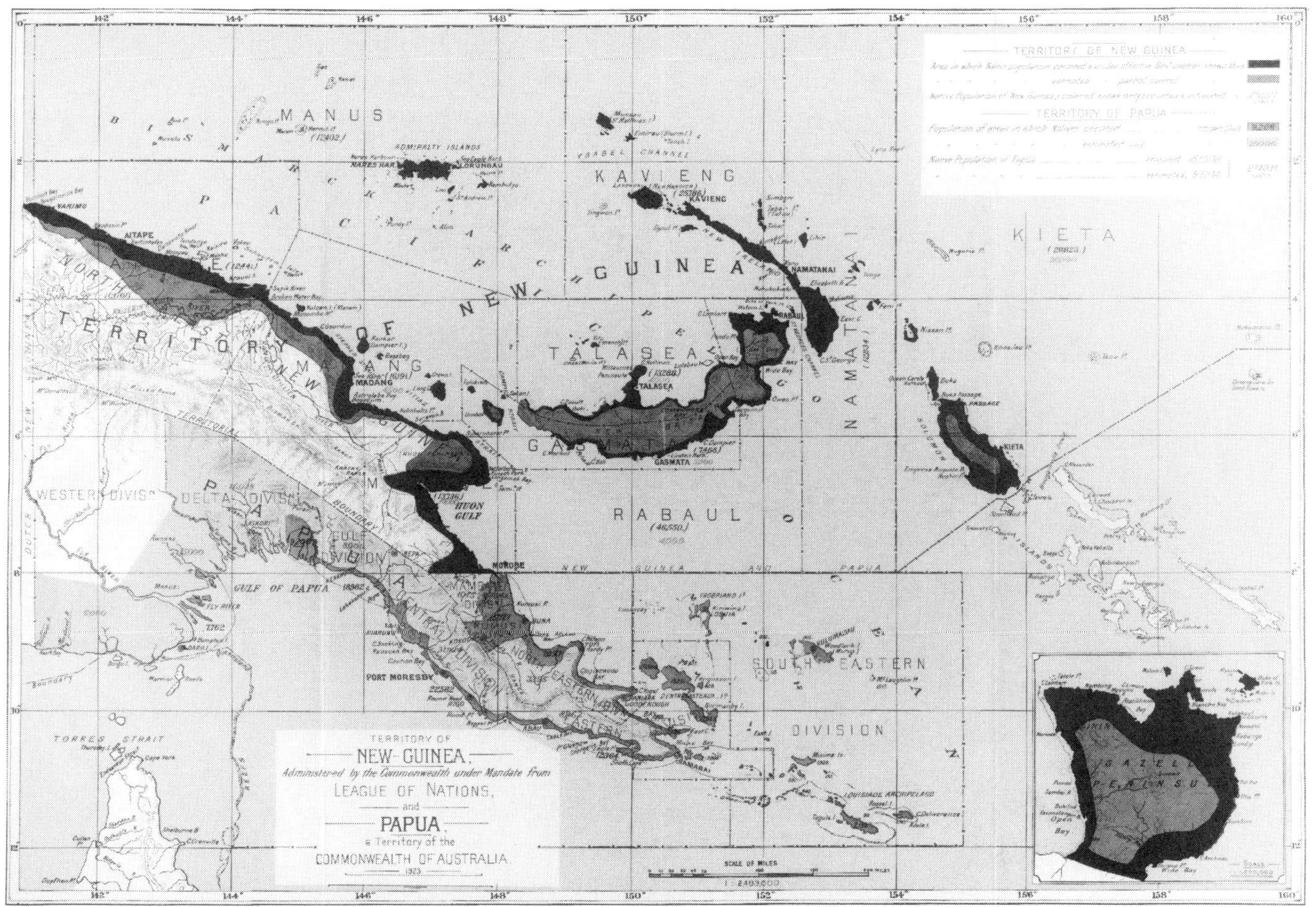

Fig. 17. Papua New Guinea. Note the importance of rivers used by European explorers as pathways into the interior. Why didn't coastal New Guineans tell Europeans of the Highland people they knew about through trading networks?

A blank space on the map

In 1920 the people of the Highlands had not seen any men with white skin. They cultivated the land, built villages and gardens and hunted in wide fertile valleys, along fast-flowing rivers and along mountain ridges. The only strangers were people from neighbouring or distant tribes who wandered across into contested territory.

Maps of Papua New Guinea drawn by Europeans in the 1920s showed a blank space over nearly half the interior. The coastline and the nearby islands had been settled by European planters and miners and there were a few European towns and settlements established on bays and rivers along the coast. Central New Guinea was assumed by the Europeans to be virtually uninhabited.

A few Europeans had glimpsed what lay in the rugged interior. Several Lutheran missionaries, a gold prospector and an Australian forestry officer had reported seeing wide fertile valleys and the smoke of many fires. Between 1926 and 1930, this seemed to indicate that there might be some *indigenous* or *native* people living in the Highlands. However, Europeans on the coast could only guess at how many — they were sure it was only a small population!

In the 1920s white men were only just entering the foothills on the fringe of the rugged highlands. The interior of New Guinea was the biggest blank space left on the globe. The age of European discovery and maritime navigation in the

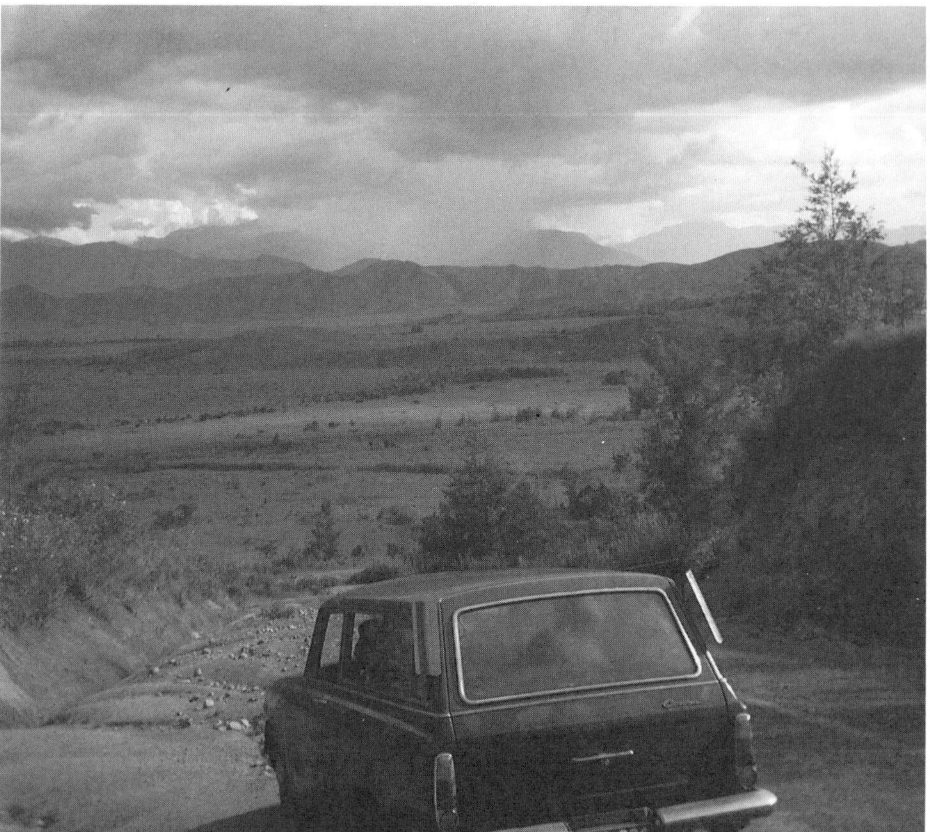

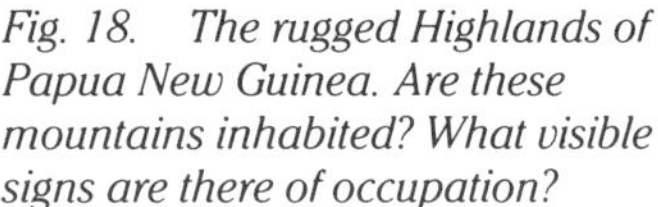

Fig. 18. The rugged Highlands of Papua New Guinea. Are these mountains inhabited? What visible signs are there of occupation?

Pacific had drawn to a close with James Cook's three great voyages (1768–1779). Most of Africa, South America and Asia had been explored and mapped and was well known. In 1930 the interior of New Guinea was therefore one of the last great challenges left for Europeans in their race to discover everything there was to know about the world. For Highlanders, their world was about to be challenged and a different type of stranger was about to enter their territory.

▲▲▲ Related questions ▲▲▲

1 Why were Europeans keen to enter the Highlands?

2 How did Europeans act towards the Highlands' people?

3 How did the Highlands' people act towards the Europeans?

ACTIVITIES

1 Do the following map work.

- **a** Draw or trace a map of Papua New Guinea (include the whole island of New Guinea).
- **b** Indicate the following places: Port Moresby, Lae, Mount Hagen, Goroka, Madang.
- **c** Indicate (by shading or lines) the location of the Highlands.

2 Make an initial assumption (this will be a guess at this stage) and complete the following sentence. 'When the Highlanders first met the Europeans they . . .'

3 Describe the landscape of Papua New Guinea using Fig. 18. How did this hinder European exploration of the area?

Practically unknown terrain

In 1932 and 1933 several pioneering aeroplane flights occurred in New Guinea. Before this the aeroplane was a new invention and was virtually unheard of in remote European settlements like those on the coasts of New Guinea. These flights allowed aviators to peer into what had been assumed to be a jumble of valleys and ridges. To their amazement they discovered an enormous population of Highlanders cultivating wide fertile valleys.

It was the combination of aerial reconnaissance and large expeditions on the ground that brought Europeans into the interior. It also brought about the first contact between Highlanders and white men.

In 1935 a young gold prospector called Jack Hides had walked through parts of the Highlands. In 1936 he cooperated with a government patrol officer, Ivan

Champion, to match his observations on the ground with what might be seen from an aeroplane. On January 24 1936, the news magazine *Pacific Islands Monthly* reported from Sydney:

> This aeroplane reconnaissance as far as we know is the first that has been attempted over this difficult and practically unknown terrain, and the result of the flight will be awaited with much interest. If it should prove to be a practical method, it probably will be used extensively in the future in securing accurate knowledge of the remaining tracts of unknown Central New Guinea.

Journalists in Sydney knew that the Dutch were using aeroplanes in the western half of New Guinea, but their assumption that this flight was the first in the Australian or eastern half of New Guinea was not correct. In March 1933 the three Leahy brothers and two others flew over the central Highlands and reported that they had:

> . . . laid to rest for all time the theory that the center of New Guinea is a mass of uninhabitable mountains. What we saw was a great flat valley possibly twenty miles wide and no telling how many miles long between two high mountains . . . below us were evidence of a fertile soil and a teeming population — a continuous patchwork of gardens laid off in neat squares like chequerboards with oblong grass houses in groups of four or five dotted thickly over the landscape . . . an island of population so effectively hemmed in by mountains that the rest of the world had not even suspected its existence.

For the explorers, aviators and journalists this was an exciting and momentous occasion. The rest of the world was 'discovering' a huge population which had never been seen by Europeans before.

The first big expeditions

The first well-equipped and well-planned expedition into the Highlands was led by Leahy and Dwyer in 1930. In 1933 this was followed by a combined expedition comprising the Leahy brothers (acting on their own account), Spinks (for the New Guinea Goldfields Company) and Jim Taylor (representing the Australian government which ruled the two territories of New Guinea and Papua at that time). In 1938–1939 a further expedition led by Taylor and Black completed the exploration and initial mapping of the Highlands.

How did Highlanders react to the arrival of these strangers? When the Highlanders realised that they could obtain desirable items of trade they began to follow the line of carriers as the Leahy expedition of 1933 slowly trekked across the countryside. They brought pigs forward and began trading. In contrast, the Sione people of the Mau valley thronged around the expedition shouting 'We turi' meaning 'men possessed by spirits'. Kirupano, an old man from the Asaroarea people, recalled that girls traded for shells that the expedition brought in from the coast. More than a thousand Chimbu people gathered on April 10 1933 when an aeroplane brought supplies to a hastily built landing strip.

Jim Taylor's opinion was that the Highlanders made few signs, of either anger or friendship. He noted that the Chimbu people were well armed but that they appeared to regard the white men in awe as something ghostly or supernatural.

Our dead ancestors were inside

The opinion of Kirupano of the Asaroarea people, who was interviewed forty years later during the making of the film *First Contact*, was as follows:

> We thought they must be our ancestors from the place of the dead. We knew nothing of the outside world. We thought we were the only people. We believed our dead went over there, turned white and came back as spirits. That's how we explained the white man.

Another Highlander who was there when the Leahy expedition arrived was Lusave. He recalled that:

> They brought a gramophone with them. They wound it up and told us to dance to its sound. We heard its cry and thought it was a box of ghosts. We thought our dead ancestors were inside. They told us to dance and we did. We thought the dead were dancing with us.

After finding out that these were normal men and that they were not a military threat, the Highlanders sought to take advantage of the situation. The guns of the white men were powerful but the expedition had only a few armed men. Using tactics from their own tribal warfare, the Highlanders teased and taunted, made obscene gestures, danced and made sudden swoops on the camp to try and grab items. Usually this resulted in a deliberate shot being fired by the exploring party and often a man was killed. The Highlanders would then withdraw.

Although they outnumbered the expedition, a few armed Europeans, with a carrier line of several hundred coastal Papuan men would still have involved a major and perhaps costly attack. Highlanders realised it was easier to gain the desired shells, salt and manufactured oddities like mirrors and beads by trading.

ACTIVITIES

1 Write answers to these questions.

- **a** In the 1933 expedition who were the three quite different groups of Europeans involved?
- **b** How long was it after 1926 before the Highlands were mapped and well known?
- **c** What evidence did the Leahy brothers use to support their first impression that there was a teeming population in the Highlands?
- **d** What military tactics did Highlanders first adopt?
- **e** What items were traded between the first expeditions and the local people?

2 Using reference books from the library, mark on your map the routes of the first European expeditions into the Highlands.

Who was the boss?

Isakoa from the Bena people recalled that Mick Leahy, who later settled in the Highlands, had a strong influence on the life of the Highlanders. Isakoa recalled, when interviewed in the 1970s: 'Masta Mick was a very hard man. He told us not to steal or spoil people's gardens, to fight amongst ourselves. He came into our territory and he was boss over us all . . .'

Today the Highlands are an important contributor to the economy of the independent nation of Papua New Guinea. They also shape much of the social, cultural and political policy of the new nation. Papua New Guinea has been an independent nation since 1975.

Recent discoveries by archaeologists show that people lived in the Highlands as early as 25 000 years ago. These first Highlanders were hunters and gatherers and practised horticulture. They also exchanged shells, stone, food and tools along well organised trade routes with tribes on the coast. Nine thousand years ago they were using drainage systems to improve their agricultural production.

Today the Highlands have been mapped by satellite and infra-red photography and seismic counters have probed the earth for minerals. The limited knowledge Europeans and Highlanders had of each other just fifty years ago, is in sharp contrast to the roads and airfields, radio and telephones, newspapers and satellites, elections for local and provincial government and a national parliament which today unite the Highlands to the rest of Papua New Guinea's three and a half million people. Today the Highlands are also experiencing the impact of mining, by both huge multinational corporations, and by indigenous 'gold diggers' searching for alluvial gold in streams and gullies once the private domain of spirits, dead ancestors and local clans.

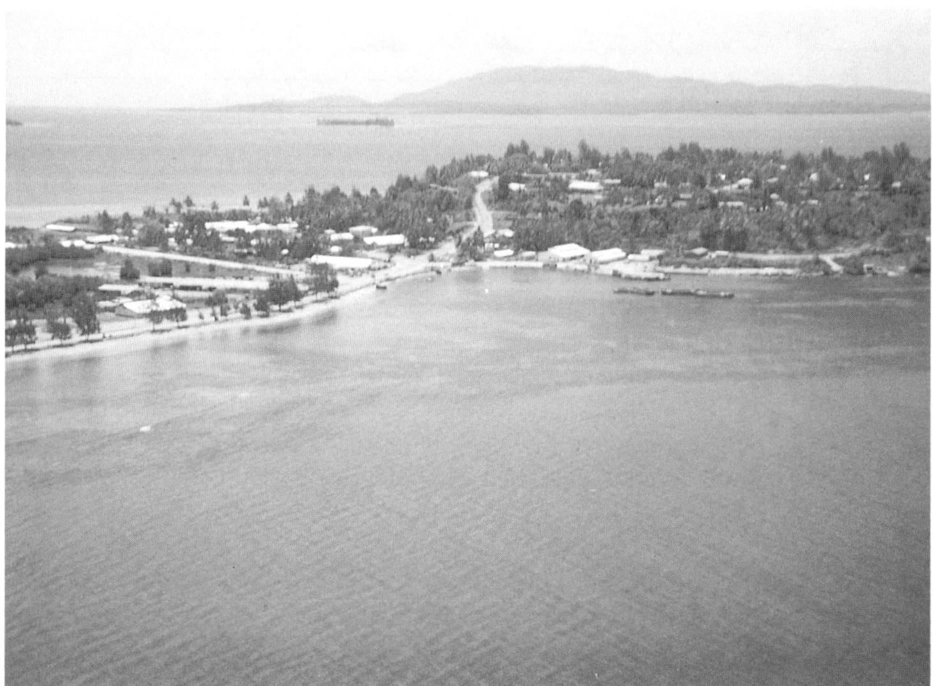

Fig. 19. A modern city in Papua New Guinea. What services does this provincial town provide? What clues might indicate the size of the population? Are there any clues on what year this photograph was taken? How would an aerial photograph of a modern Highlands town differ from this one?

ACTIVITIES

1 Answer these questions giving your own opinion.
   - **a** Why do you think the aeroplane was not used before 1930 on surveying flights?
   - **b** Why do you think it took so long for Europeans to finally map Central New Guinea?
   - **c** What events in Australia or the rest of the world might have affected the desire of Europeans to find what Central New Guinea was like?
   - **d** Why do you think *Pacific Islands Monthly* mistakenly claimed in 1936 that the first reconnaissance flight was about to occur, when an aeroplane had been used at least three years before?

2 Look back at the assumptions you made in question 4 on p. 35.
   - **a** Rewrite your initial statement or sentence.
   - **b** Add a second or third sentence if you need to say more.
   - **c** Read it to a partner. Ask their opinion on what you have written.
   - **d** Rewrite after making further changes.
   - **e** Write this statement on the sheet with your map. Pin it on the board or display area of the classroom. This is your final statement.

RESEARCH PROJECTS

1 Look up the names of Jack Hides, Mick Leahy, Jim Taylor and Ivan Champion in the *Australian Dictionary of Biography* or an encyclopaedia. What additional information do these references provide about the first Europeans in Central New Guinea?

2 Who was first? Research and then write a similar story on who was the first European into another area, for example:
   - ▲ the Amazon basin
   - ▲ Antarctica
   - ▲ China
   - ▲ Central Australia

3 Research what happened in the Highlands in the twenty years following the expeditions of 1926–1939. Draw a timeline showing other major events in the lives of the Highlanders between 1939 and 1990.

4 Read Gavin Souter's book *New Guinea: The Last Unknown*.

5 Listen to Parts 13, 14 and 15 of the ABC (Australian Broadcasting Corporation) radio series 'Taim Bilong Masta'.

6 In 1987 a new book on this topic was released, *First Contact* by Bob Connolly and Robin Anderson. What does it say about the attitudes and behaviour of the Highlanders?

Resources

Connolly B. & Anderson R. *First Contact*, Viking, 1987.
'First Contact' (Review), *Pacific Islands Monthly*, April 1988, p. 26.
First Contact, Ronin Films, Canberra, 16 mm and video.
Griffin, J. 'First contact in New Guinea highlands', *Hemisphere*, vol 29, no. 1, 1984.
Nelson, H. *Taim Bilong Masta*, Chs 13, 14 & 15, ABC Books.
Souter, G. *New Guinea: The Last Unknown*, Ch. 13, Angus and Robertson, Sydney, 1967.
'Taim Bilong Masta', ABC radio series. (Available on 12 audio cassettes.)

People on the Move: Relocation and Resettlement

5

Focus question

Why do Pacific Islanders travel regularly and for long periods within their own area, nation, region and beyond?

Making a new home

In the 1930s on the atoll of Beru in southern Kiribati (previously called the Gilbert Islands) a family with six children admitted that their only food supply was twenty coconut trees, whatever fish they could catch, and 'begging in the day and thieving at night'.

Many others were living in poverty in overcrowded communities in the southern atolls. A large number of unsettled disputes over land claims and land

Fig. 20. What kinds of natural resources would be available on an atoll in the Pacific?

titles (more than 70 000 claims were being disputed) meant these families had little prospect of gaining enough land to support themselves. When the government investigated the possibility of a migration scheme to help ease the overcrowding, a petition was sent from Beru signed by 750 people (nearly half the population) hopeful of moving.

More than 6500 applications were eventually received from the seven southern atolls in Kiribati. Between December 1938 and September 1940 (the scheme was suspended during the Second World War) 729 people moved from southern Kiribati to three uninhabited atolls in the Phoenix Islands.

Mobility has always played a major part in Pacific Islands lifestyles. From their very first contact with European shipping, Islanders were willing to sign on for voyages to unknown destinations, often for periods of more than three years. Islanders also moved to the coast to acquire European goods by working at coastal trading depots and ports. In the 19th century many had gone to Hawaii, Tahiti, Fiji or Queensland as labour recruits, or had worked for short periods on other islands as divers, sandalwood cutters, and pilots. Many had travelled for 'fun' or from curiosity. This willingness to travel was perhaps a continuation of their ancient voyaging and long-distance navigation traditions.

Planned migration like the Phoenix Island scheme may be contrasted to the voluntary relocation of Tuvaluans to Kioa Island in Fiji, and the forced relocation of Banabans to Rabi Island in Fiji, or of Bikinians to Ejit, Kili and Majuro Atolls.

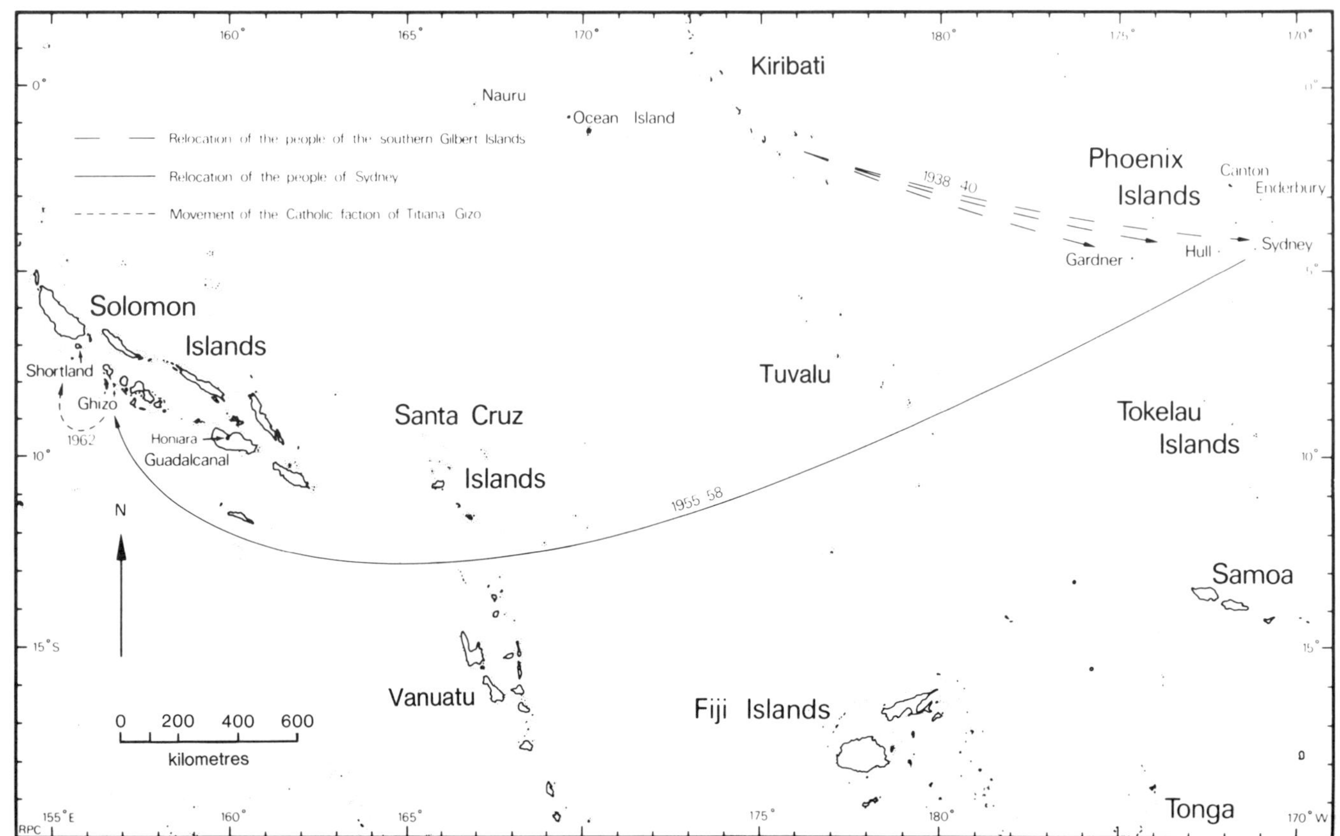

Fig. 21. This map shows major migrations from Kiribati to the Solomon Islands. What other minor movements of people could be added?

These Islanders left their homes and have not returned. Other types of migration in the Pacific have involved smaller voluntary groups leaving their traditional land and homelands. For example, there is a Niuean community in Western Samoa, an Ambrym community in Vanuatu and a Tikopean community on Russell Island.

Other migrations occur internally as outer island people move closer to the main island, major port or capital city. For example, in the Cook Islands there is a Tongarevan community on Rarotonga. Landless and temporary migrants have also moved in large numbers to the fringes of cities to become squatters. Behind the town of Honiara in the Solomon Islands there are sixteen squatter villages, containing 500 houses and nearly 2000 people. There are also those who move for long-term or short-term work, education or training to different villages, islands, or countries. For example, there are at least 20 000 Papua New Guineans away from home working on government projects. Many sign on as crew on board ships. Finally there are those who still call themselves Tongans, Samoans or Cook Islanders but who live in New Zealand, Australia, Hawaii, Canada or the United States of America. For example, more Niueans live in New Zealand than in Niue.

Resettlement and mobility, whether forced or voluntary, planned or unplanned, short-term or long-term, internal or external, is a major theme in the history of the Pacific in the 20th century.

▲▲▲ Related questions ▲▲▲

1 Why have Islanders been so willing to travel?

2 What have been the consequences of planned migrations?

3 What have been the causes of squatting?

4 How do Islanders who have resettled maintain contacts with their traditional home, family and culture?

5 What policies can governments introduce to slow the process of urban drift?

6 Why is short-term internal and regional labour migration so popular?

7 How well have original local communities accepted migrant resettlement schemes which have been established nearby?

8 Is migration an answer to Pacific Island over-population?

9 What problems are caused by a population loss to 'western' rim nations?

ACTIVITIES

Leave some space in your notebooks between each activity as you will return later to make alterations and add more information.

1 Draft a letter from the Beru Atoll people to the organiser of the 1930 Kiribati migration scheme and list the basic requirements needed for the new island home. Consider flora, fauna, and other environmental features.

2 List the jobs to be carried out by the exploration party that will first go to the Phoenix Islands to see if they are suitable for migration.

3 Draw up a list of rules for the people who are going, including
- ▲ rules which affect their status on the island they will be leaving
- ▲ rules affecting the voyage out
- ▲ rules affecting the first three months on the new island

4 Draw up a timeline of tasks for the first three months. Indicate
- ▲ the jobs to be done
- ▲ the order in which they should be carried out
- ▲ the expected length of time to complete each task

Manra, Titiana and New Manra

The population of southern Kiribati had remained constant for nearly a century. The population was finely balanced against the food supply which the atoll's scarce resources could supply. Infanticide, warfare, abortion and immigration to neighbouring atolls had traditionally kept the population balanced against food resources. However, in the late 19th and early 20th centuries, centralised government control, improved medical conditions and mission influence affected all four control mechanisms and upset this balance. Poverty and overcrowding resulted.

When a new home was being considered for people from crowded southern Kiribati, twenty-three possible atolls were identified. They were all British possessions as the Kiribati wanted to remain under British rule. It was felt that a fertile, volcanic island would be too different so the choice had to be a coral atoll. Coral atolls like those in southern Kiribati were typically flat (often less than 3 metres above sea-level), with limited soil, limited natural vegetation and fauna, little rain, and with poor access for large ships. But this was the type of lifestyle the people preferred; fishing in lagoons and the open ocean and cultivating coconut palms and planting babai — the root crop which grows sparsely and needs great care and attention.

The Phoenix Islands to the east of Kiribati were chosen as the site for the migration scheme. A team was sent to prepare the way for the main migration

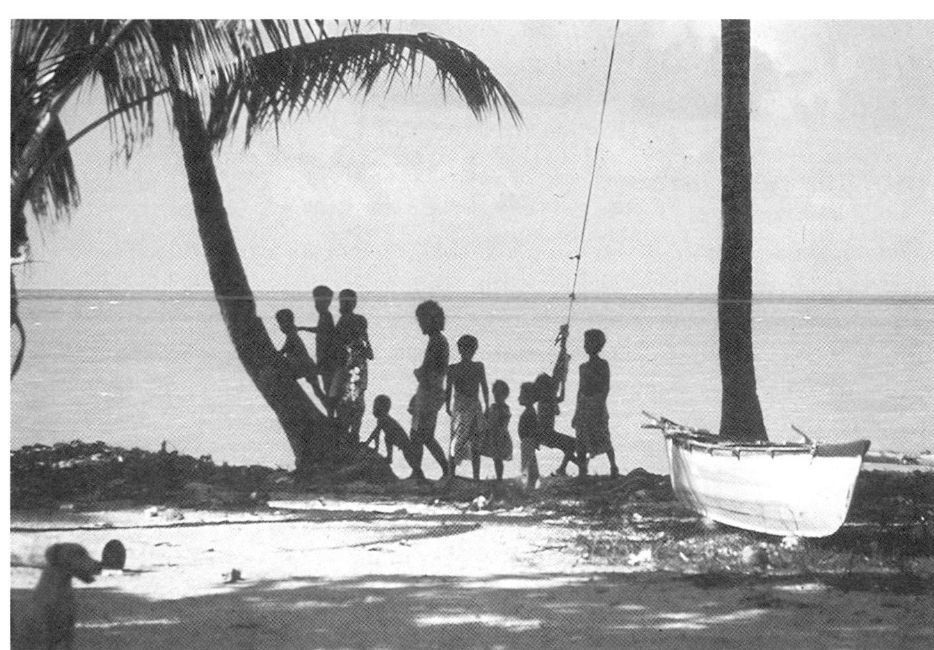

Fig. 22. A Pacific atoll. Is it possible to estimate a maximum population density for an atoll like this? Is land size important? What other factors should be considered?

party. The Phoenix Islands were then uninhabited. They had a similar climate, topography and flora and fauna. At various times they had been used for coconut plantations, stopovers on ancient voyages and for short fishing expeditions.

The exploring party which preceded the migration feasted on crabs and booby birds, caught fish in their bare hands in the lagoon, dug wells to test for water, surveyed land for government buildings and village sites and made an inventory of all fruit-bearing trees. Landing sites for cargo and mail were chosen, pathways pegged and the British flag raised.

In December 1938 the first families landed on the three Phoenix Islands. They were renamed Orona, Manra and Nikumaroro. By 1951 the population had increased to one thousand and the scheme was judged a great success. Only seven people had been returned to their former home (for crimes and homesickness).

The first settlers eagerly tackled the many tasks of making the uninhabited atolls habitable. Plots of land were allocated, seeds planted, food plantations started, permanent housing soon replaced tents (using both local materials and timber and mats brought with them). Decisions were made on how major work, such as clearing the bush, would be tackled. One village decided on a community work scheme with equal contributions so that in return everyone could rely on others for help when it was needed. The other village on Manra chose to work individually within each family, and to pay others for help when it was needed. Community dancing and singing, a young men's club, a community meeting house, a guesthouse for official visitors, a prison and a church soon appeared. Later some travelled to the nearby airbase on Canton Island, or to coconut plantations in the nearby Line Islands and obtained temporary employment. Despite the isolation during the war, government officials reported in 1950 that the migrants were enjoying their new home.

Within a few years the situation changed dramatically. A split developed between the Catholic and Protestant communities, and poor fishing and serious droughts made life on the three atolls precarious.

Another new home

Between 1955 and 1958 the people of Manra moved again, this time to the village of Titiana on Ghizo Island in the Solomon Islands. The Solomon Islands were also a British colony at this time. It was suggested that a migration of Kiribati to the Solomon Islands would solve a labour shortage problem in the Solomons, as well as solving overcrowding in southern Kiribati and the settlers' problems in the Phoenix Islands.

In 1963 the people on Orono and Nikumaroro also moved, to Wagina (Vaghena) in the Solomon Islands. The Phoenix Islands were once again uninhabited. Meanwhile in the Solomons, some of those who had settled at Titiana moved again to nearby off-shore islands and to the Shortland Islands, just north of Ghizo.

The Kiribati community on Ghizo established their new village at Titiana. In 1958 the growing population (2.6 per cent per annum) and further migration led to another village, New Manra, being established about a kilometre closer to the

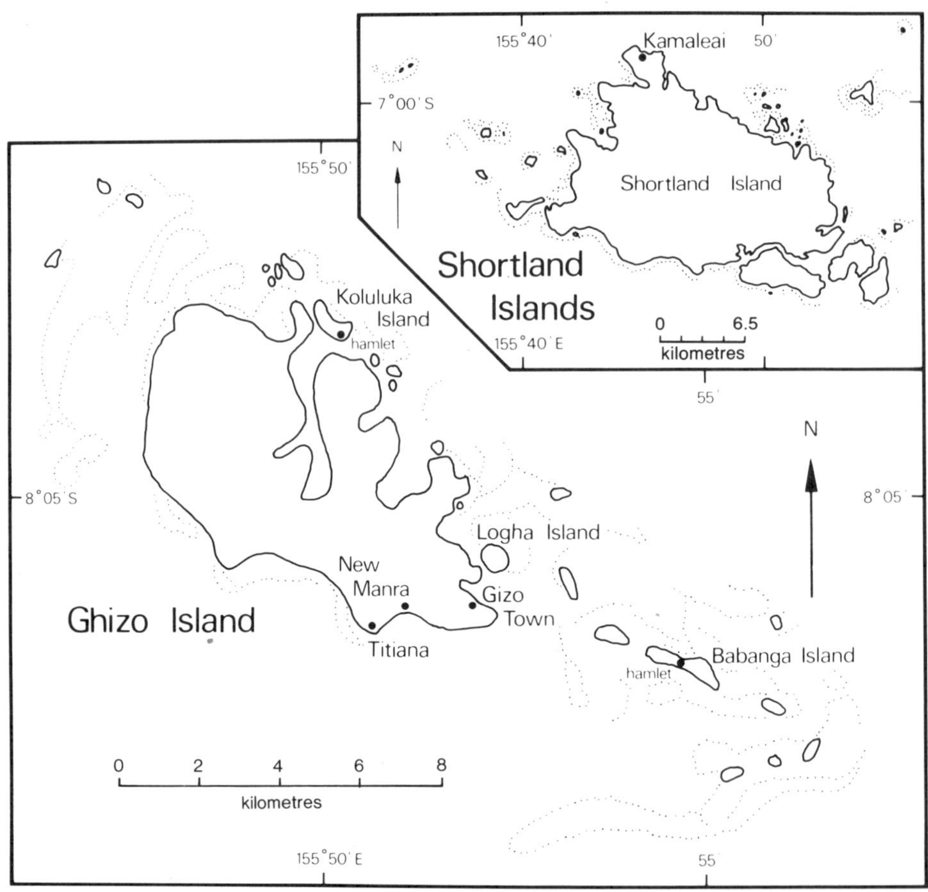

Fig. 23. Destination islands: Ghizo and the Shortland Islands.

main port on Ghizo. Some Catholic members of the community later moved to Logha Island also near Ghizo, or to the Shortland Islands. A Kiribati community was also established near Honiara, the capital city of the Solomon Islands, and on Babanga Island, just south of Ghizo. By 1970 there were 2362 Kiribati living in these dispersed locations around the Solomon Islands.

ACTIVITY

Write answers to these questions.

a How many atolls are there in Kiribati?
b Describe a typical atoll in about fifty words. (See Figs 20 and 22.)
c What were the four 'mechanisms' that enabled atoll populations to be kept in balance with the food supply?
d What is babai?
e Why were the Phoenix Islands chosen as the site for migration from Kiribati?
f What buildings did the new migrants construct in the Phoenix Islands?
g What opportunities existed for the migrants to earn money?
h When did the Manra settlers move to the Solomon Islands?
i What five locations in the Solomons did Kiribati migrants eventually settle in?
j After the settlement at Titiana in 1955, why did the other movements within the Solomons occur?

Custom, land and two cultures

Relations between the Kiribati and Solomon Islanders were neither close nor hostile. If problems arose they usually involved the ownership of land. The migrants had been promised individual ownership of land for housing and farming. Many Solomon Islanders resented this. Although there is some individual ownership, most Solomon Islanders do not individually own a piece of land. It usually 'belongs' to a traditional family or kinship group, or is leased from the government.

When the Solomon Islands were approaching independence in 1979 land ownership became a big issue. Some Solomon Islanders feared the Kiribati would become a separate, rich land-owning class, or would take the few well-paid government jobs available and end up better off than the Solomon Islanders. This has not happened. Intermarriage has occurred, Solomon Islanders have settled in the Kiribati villages and the Kiribati have been absorbed into the Solomon Islands work-force in the timber industry or on government cattle ranch schemes. Many have joined Solomon Islanders in jobs in the nearby towns and cities. Annual Kiribati singing and dancing competitions, traditional Kiribati marriage ceremonies and other feasts and ceremonies have continued but have gradually become less and less popular.

Titiana and New Manra, which are near the major port and city on Ghizo Island, have been absorbed into the mainstream of Solomon Islands lifestyles. The people there have become urbanised and have moved away from their former Kiribati subsistence farming and fishing lifestyle. In contrast, because of their remoteness from an urban centre, those who moved to the Shortland Islands well to the north of Ghizo, have maintained more closely their Kiribati customs and traditions.

Like other communities in the Pacific, and migrants everywhere that have found a new home, Kiribati children born in the Solomon Islands now have two cultures, and two ways of life to follow. Voyce Pitakaka, a Solomon Islander wrote in 1979 that Solomon Islands politicians:

> . . . should say strongly that the Gilbertese [Kiribati] settlers can continue to own the land they have, and that their children should have equal rights with other Solomon Islanders. This way we will avoid conflict between us and face the hardships of independence together.

ACTIVITIES

1 Read your answer to question 1 on p. 44 again. Draft a new letter, including information you know is important, to people joining a migration scheme.

2 Reconsider your answer to question 2 on p. 44. Check the list of jobs you thought the exploration party would have to carry out. Add any further information you now have, and then number the tasks in order of priority.

3 Re-examine your answer to question 4 on p. 44. Check the list of jobs you thought the settlers would do in the first three months. Add any further information you now have. Renumber the tasks in order of priority and alter the timing taken for each task (if necessary).

4 Answer these questions giving your own opinion.

- **a** Why do you think people who had been desperate for land and had chosen to settle in a new home in the Phoenix Islands, would then travel to other islands in search of paid work?
- **b** Why is land ownership or access to land so important in Pacific Island resettlement schemes?
- **c** Do you think the Solomon Islands' government should give permanent, individual land ownership to Kiribati settlers?
- **d** What policies and attractive offers can governments introduce to convince Pacific Islanders that they should not migrate and 'squat' near big cities?

RESEARCH PROJECTS

1 On a map of the Pacific mark in with broad arrows, using different colours, the following migrations. Include the dates.

- ▲ Beru (Kiribati) to Manra (Phoenix) to Gizo (Solomon Islands) from 1938 to 1955–57.
- ▲ Niue to Western Samoa in 1938
- ▲ Banaba to Rabi (Fiji) in 1946
- ▲ Bikini to Rongerik, Kwajalein and Kili (all Marshall Islands) in 1946
- ▲ Tuvalu to Kioa (Fiji) in 1947
- ▲ Tikopia to Russell Island (Solomon Islands) in 1949

2 Read the book *The Fire has Jumped*, Garth Rogers (ed.) on resettlement after a volcanic eruption on Niuafo'ou Island, Tonga.

3 After the Second World War Bikini Atoll was used for nuclear testing. Assuming that the Bikini Atoll people can no longer return home (due to continuing nuclear radiation on Bikini) what should be done to help them resettle somewhere else? Watch the videos and films on Bikini Islander resettlement: *Half Life, Living with the Bomb, Radio Bikini* or *Atomic Cafe*.

4 Forced repatriation made international headlines in 1989 when Hong Kong forced Vietnam refugees on to a ship and returned them to Vietnam. Why were the British criticised? Were the refugees welcomed back? Why/why not? What impact would forced repatriation have on people of the Pacific?

5 Interview any person who has recently migrated. Discuss whether it was planned, voluntary, forced or 'luck' that made them choose their new home. What is their relationship with their old home? Do they still own land there? Do they own land in their new home? Is the ownership of land important to them?

Resources

Chapman, M. (ed.) 'Mobility and identity in the Island Pacific', *Pacific Viewpoint*, vol 26, no. 1, 1985.

Leiber, M. (ed.) *Exiles and Migrants in Oceania*, University of Hawaii Press, Honolulu, 1977.

Mason, L. & Hereniko, P. (eds) *In Search of a Home*, USP/Institute for Pacific Studies, Suva, 1987.

Maude, H. *Of Islands and Men*, Ch. 8, Oxford University Press, Melbourne, 1968.

Waita, B. *et al. Land in the Solomon Islands*, USP/Institute for Pacific Studies, Suva, 1979.

Pacific Islands Monthly and *Pacific Business* have regular articles on mobility, migration and settlement schemes.

6 The War in the Pacific: 'We have got nothing'

Focus question

How did invasion and occupation during the Second World War affect Pacific Islanders?

'We just live our own lives, that's all'

When the Second World War was over, Yauwiga, a young man from the East Sepik region of Papua New Guinea, had an artificial arm and was blind in both eyes. He was awarded a Distinguished Conduct Medal (DCM); it was his reward for gallant service during the war.

Just before he died in 1981 he said that before the war in Papua New Guinea his people had not made:

> . . . things for fighting wars with other countries. We just grow our own food and have sing-sings and beat our drums, that's all. We don't know how to make warships or submarines, bombs or bullets. We just live our own lives, that's all.

In the central Pacific on the atoll of Funafuti in the Tuvalu Islands, the impact of the war in 1941 also prevented people from just living their own lives. Neli Lifuka remembered that in 1941 'we heard the planes. We were scared. My heart was beating but I didn't know what to do'. Although Tuvalu was only used as a staging depot by American troops, Funafuti was bombed seven times between March and November 1943. When writing his life story Neli Lifuka recalled:

> . . . after some time we were no longer scared about the bombing. When we heard the siren we just went to our foxholes but didn't go down until they started dropping bombs. We watched the planes and swore at them.

Neli also recalls seeing bigger and more ships in the harbour than he had ever seen before. Forty-three ships arrived in October 1943 and 174 in January 1944. Suddenly there were as many as 6000 Americans on Funafuti, Nanumea and Nukufetau, the three atolls they occupied. The Americans are remembered fondly as good visitors.

The Tuvalans and Americans worked together on airstrips and supply depots, but other relationships were strictly controlled. When they wrote a history of their atolls, thirty years after the war, Tuvalans recalled that only four part-American children were born. Neli Lifuka recalled the equality and friendships

Fig. 24. Are these men invaders, strangers, employers, benefactors or friends?

and having breakfast with the soldiers. 'We always ate together, we had the same food. We mixed like that with the Americans.' Early in 1945 all the men and equipment were just as suddenly gone.

For the people of Oria on Bougainville Island in the Solomon Islands the war was a more tragic experience. After they landed in 1942 the Japanese had recruited some local villagers for labour. But other villagers, loyal to British and Australian coastwatching officials, attacked Japanese patrols for the next three years. When the Australians, Fijians and Americans landed at Torokina on the west coast and began a counter-offensive, the number of attacks increased. In April 1945 ten men from Oria were asked to go to the Japanese camp to be paid for their work. Instead they were fired upon. Seven were killed. The other three were wounded but escaped. Solomon Islanders also recall that Australian coastwatchers had executed Bougainvillians who had committed 'treason' by aiding the enemy.

The immediate impact of the war on Bougainville Island was dramatic. The Bougainvillians had seen most of their former 'masters' flee to safety — the planters, missionaries and government officials. In contrast, the Japanese when they arrived in March 1942 had initially adopted a friendly attitude, and were scrupulous about paying for foodstuffs and labour and in punishing soldiers for molesting local women.

In the rugged interior of Bougainville Island, away from the main campaigns of the war, the villagers suffered a shortage of 'trade goods' but were otherwise unaffected. In the atolls of Kiribati a similar variation in impact occurred. Only three atolls were 'occupied'. On the other thirteen atolls the main impact was that imported goods such as kerosene, tinned foods and manufactured tools became scarce. Islanders recalled that tobacco was greatly missed, particularly by the old men and women and that instead of cotton or woollen shirts, dresses and shorts, people reverted to wearing grass skirts.

In some places the war did reach deep into all aspects of people's lives. Among the Toaripi villagers of the Gulf of Papua, the whole population was concerned in some way with the war effort. A government official reported that the Toaripis' 'village life is totally disrupted'. Although it was outside the fighting zone of the war, due to conscription and demands on the remaining men and women to supply housing and building materials and food, and even their canoes, all were affected.

Chris Perez Howard from Guam in the northern Pacific, whose father spent 1365 days in captivity, and whose mother was murdered by occupation forces, has written that 'in the war between the United States of America and Japan, the peaceful and hospitable people of Guam were the losers'.

▲▲▲ Related questions ▲▲▲

1 Which islands were affected by military occupation?

2 Who invaded, when, and for how long did military action last?

3 How were Islanders living outside the campaign perimeters affected?

4 What was the political status of the Islanders before the war arrived?

5 How did war experiences change Islanders' attitudes towards their former 'masters'?

6 What were the policies of the invading forces regarding contact with local people?

7 What are the opinions of Islanders about their treatment during the war, and after the war?

ACTIVITIES

1 Write a single statement of four words, imagining that it will be used as a front page banner headline in a newspaper on the day after the arrival of the Japanese on Bougainville. Write a headline statement for each of the following:
- ▲ a newspaper published in Kieta (main town) on Bougainville Island
- ▲ a newspaper published in Tokyo, Japan
- ▲ a newspaper published in Brisbane, Australia

2 List the possible actions that a villager might take upon learning that a number of 'foreigners' have occupied a large part of the nearby coast and that the former 'masters' have fled from the island. List at least ten options. (These options will be guesses at this stage.)

3 Write a message of about fifty words, imagining that you are the current government official in charge of Bougainville in 1942. The message is to go to all villagers explaining what they should do when the Japanese arrive. Remember that many of the villagers will have a limited understanding of the English language.

'I thought of nothing else'

At the peak of the fighting on Bougainville there were 65 000 Japanese troops on the island. In November 1943, when American forces landed at Torokina on the west coast, another 40 000 foreigners were present. The allied forces also included Australians and two battalions of Fijian soldiers. The Americans established three airstrips, a naval base, saw mills, generating plants, storage dumps, workshops, hospitals, 112 kilometres of road, gardens, sports ovals and theatres for films and live performances.

Fig. 25. The wreck of a warship used during the Second World War. What impact did new technology have on people caught in combat zones? What long-term changes in technology might have occurred because of the war? Were people in the islands left 'emply-handed' when the war ended?

The impact on Islanders caught inside the American or the Japanese combat perimeter was profound. The historian Hank Nelson has described their predicament: 'They had no choice; they obeyed those who were present and held the guns'. Other Islanders were living, soon precariously, between the opposing armies:

> . . . the people occupying the lands between the contending armies had to make choices, and they were choices that could determine what would happen to their property and their lives. They had to make decisions on the basis of very little knowledge.

For example, on the atoll of Butaritari in the Kiribati Islands, during the American invasion, three drunk Islanders, unaware of what was happening, were killed in the bombing as the Americans landed, and another, who misunderstood the advice shouted to him, was killed in crossfire between the opposing forces.

The First World War (1914–1918) had barely affected the Pacific Islands. In comparison the impact of the Pacific campaigns (1941–1945) of the Second World War was profound in places suddenly caught in the middle of a combat zone.

In non-combat zones near the fighting the impact was often just as great. In the Gulf of Papua, for example, where no military campaigns were fought, the full impact was felt for all four years of the Pacific War. Islands well outside the war zone, but used as depots and supply areas, also felt the impact of new technology and huge numbers of 'foreigners'.

The violence of the war passed quickly for some. Funafuti Atoll was bombed seven times early in 1943 but then peace returned as the war moved west and northwards. For most Solomon Islanders the fighting lasted only two years. In

Fig. 26. War-time campaigns on Buka and Bougainville Islands. Does this map indicate the human cost to the people who occupied this zone in the war?

contrast, in Papua New Guinea, the Japanese occupation of the north-west coast, Manus Island and New Britain lasted four years.

The military maps drawn by the generals, with arrows and heavy black lines symbolising advances and retreats, do not show the human cost to the people who occupied the black dots (un-named villages), ridges and valleys through

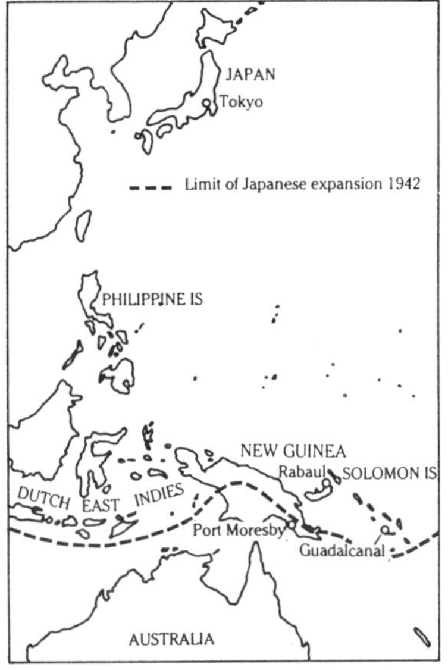

Fig. 27. The war in New Guinea, 1942. Is this map useful for judging the impact of the war? What other information is needed on the area occupied, the area not occupied and about each island in order to establish the effect of the war on the population?

which the war travelled. This human cost can be measured by 'native' deaths as the result of combat or military action. It must also be measured by the changes imposed on customary lifestyles. The diet, birth rates, crop fertility, marriages, and ancestor worship changed due to the presence of a huge, foreign and often inexplicable invasion of men, technology and alien forms of behaviour.

In Papua New Guinea there may have been as many as 40 000 villagers killed. In just one small area, the Tolai Peninsula of New Britain Island, 7000 villagers were killed. At the other end of the scale, in the central Pacific atolls of Kiribati, two Islanders were killed in the American amphibious invasion of Tarawa Atoll and four killed in the invasion of Butaritari Atoll. Forty-one Butaritari people were also killed during a mis-timed aerial bombing of the atoll and more than a hundred phosphate workers were executed on Ocean Island (Banaba) towards the end of the war. On Funafuti Atoll two deaths occurred, one during a bombing raid and the other when a man was accidentally shot for breaking a night-time beach curfew.

On the Tolai Peninsula of the island of New Britain, during the invasion, the death rate among children under five years was as high as 40 per cent. Among the inland tribes behind the Aitape coast of Papua New Guinea it was thought that 35 per cent of the people had been affected by the battles. In the two inland village clusters of the Urat and Urim people, 1400 died due to military action. However, as many as three times this number probably died of medical neglect, disease (such as dysentery and smallpox) and psychological stress related to the war's impact.

Fig. 28. The American invasion of Tarawa, November 1943 — a typical map.

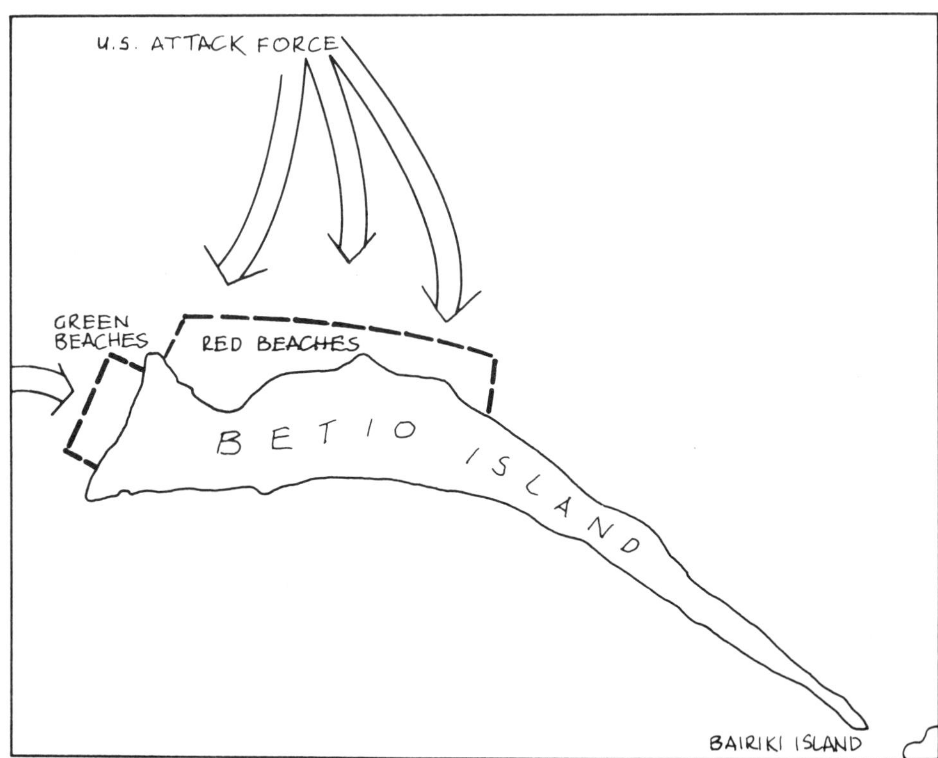

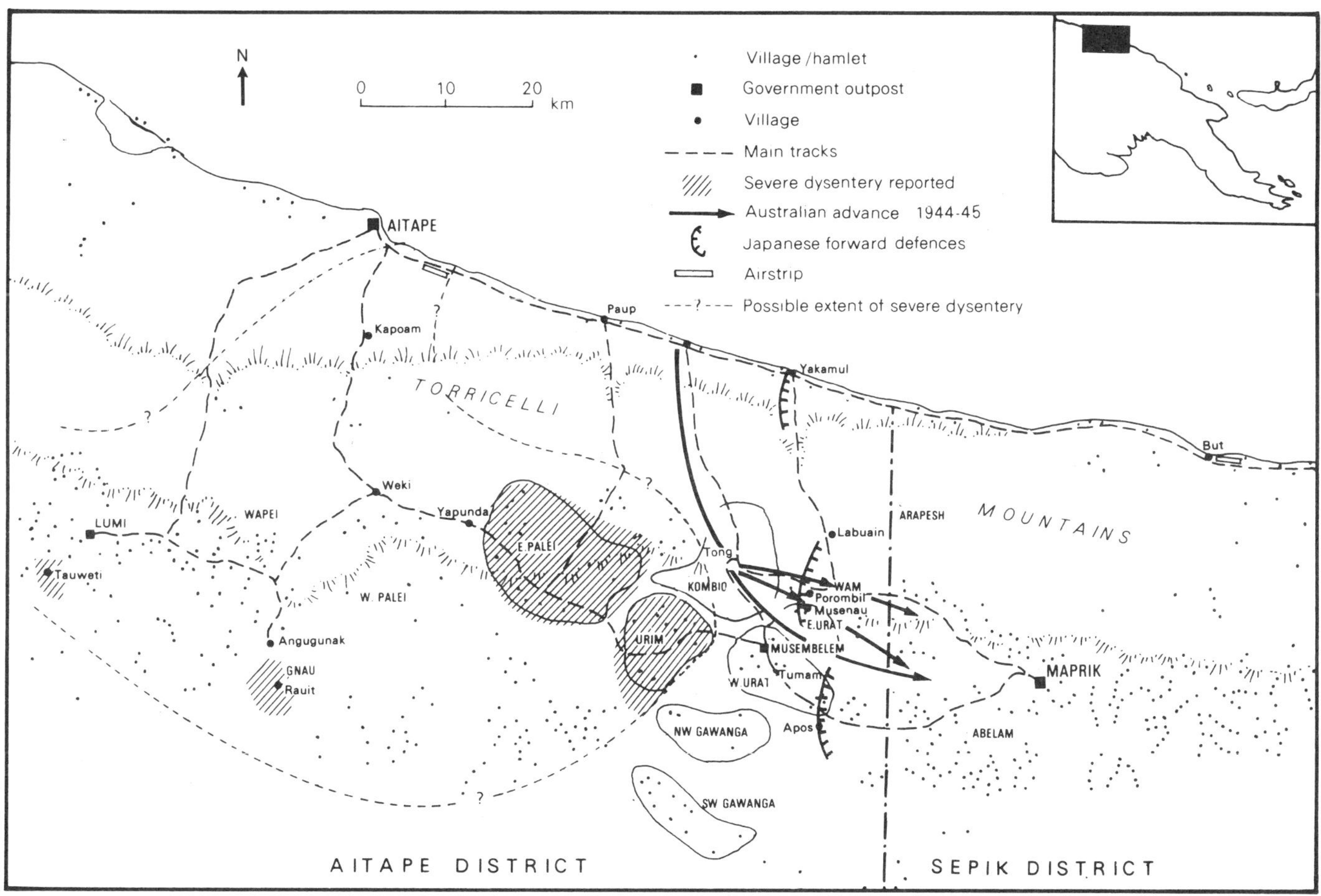

Fig. 29. The Aitape and Sepik districts in Papua New Guinea during the Second World War.

Stress meant that many nursing mothers were unable to breast feed their children. For many the will to live was challenged by traumatic events beyond the control of their normally powerful spirits, gods and totems. Lowered resistance to disease and inadequate food supplies resulted when people had to move from villages high on ridge lines, and near their gardens and food supplies, to go into hiding in the darker, stagnant, wetter valleys.

Day to day contact with the occupying forces also varied. Many Islanders worked with their invaders, collaborating or working as labourers, guides and helpers. In other occupied areas, those who could moved away from the military camps and patrol posts.

Others were conscripted into labour gangs on their own island or in distant and foreign islands. On Funafuti Atoll, 200 labourers worked at an American supply base, and on Nanumea Atoll 80 men worked as divers to place explosives and blast passages through the reef around the atoll. In Kiribati, 1200 men joined the Labour Corps as they were known, and later 400 were sent to Guadalcanal in the Solomon Islands to work. In the Solomon Islands, at the peak of the war, there were about 2500 men in the Solomon Islands Labour Corps. In Papua New Guinea as many as 50 000 men were working for the Allies at the peak of the fighting, and an unknown number for the Japanese. These figures do not include women and adolescents who also worked temporarily for an invading force.

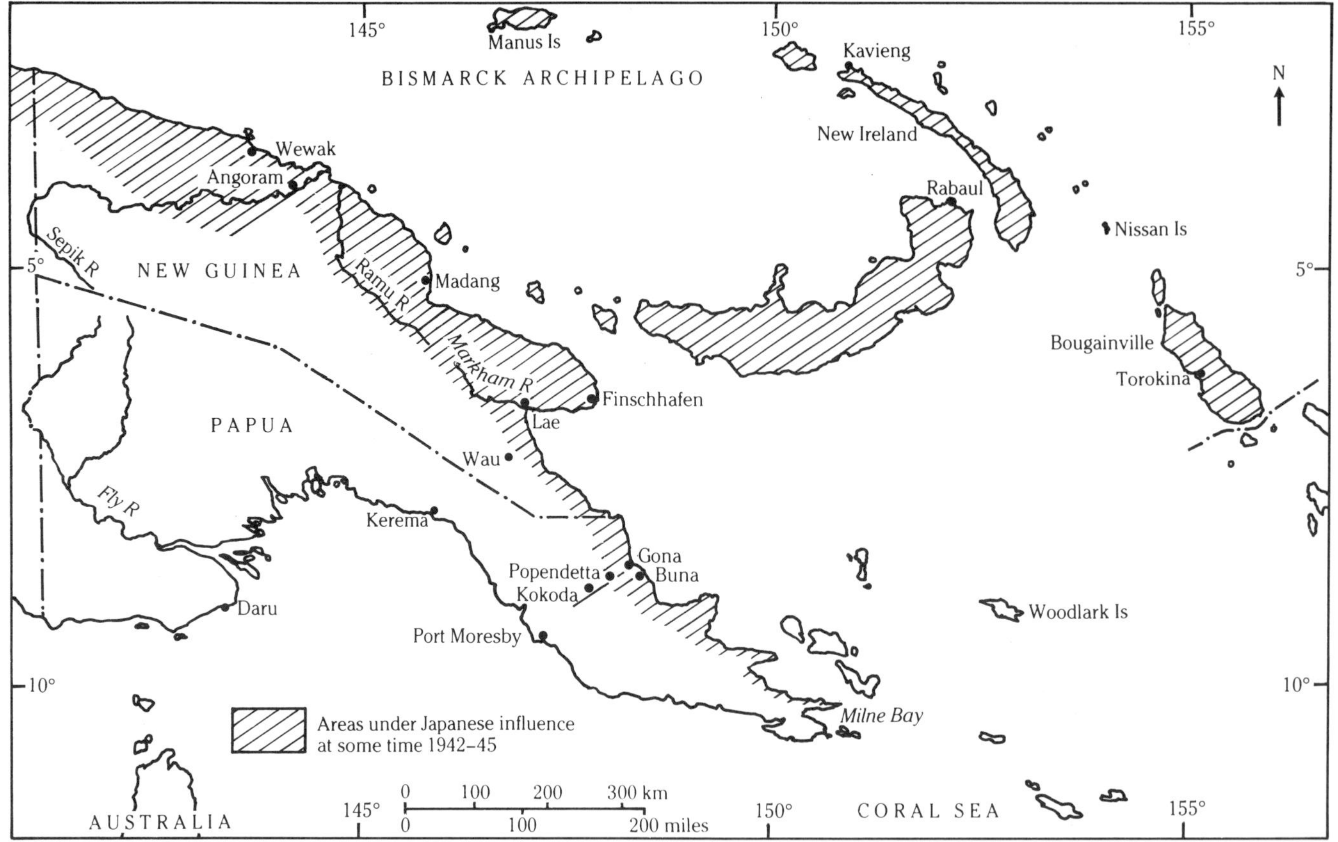

Fig. 30. Japanese presence in Papua New Guinea during the Second World War.

In the Solomon Islands and Papua New Guinea many villagers served as combat troops, or unofficially in guerilla-type operations. Five thousand Papua New Guineans also served as combat troops in the newly created Pacific Islands regiment. Three thousand served as military policemen and 995 as medical orderlies. From outside the war zone, in Fiji, 1700 Fijians who had signed up during the war were sent to the Solomons and served as combat troops against the Japanese. One was posthumously awarded the Victoria Cross (VC). Fifty-seven Fijians died during the campaign.

The war remains a major passage in the history of the Pacific. Indeed for many years the pidgin English phrase 'taem bipo' was used to divide time into two periods, before and after the war.

ACTIVITIES

1 Write answers to these questions.

a How many times was Funafuti Atoll bombed during the war?

b How many foreign troops were on Bougainville Island at the peak of the fighting?

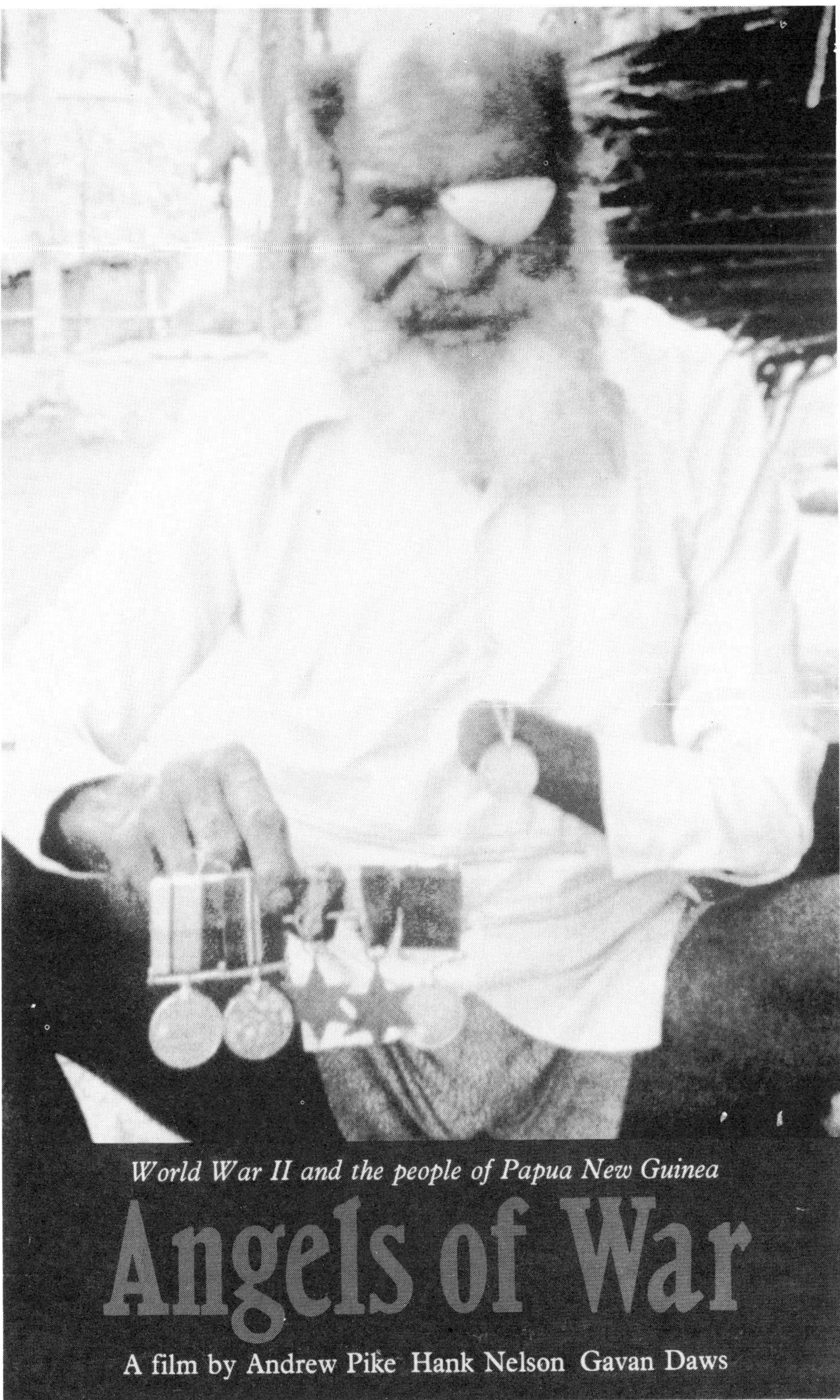

World War II and the people of Papua New Guinea
Angels of War
A film by Andrew Pike Hank Nelson Gavan Daws

Fig. 31. A poster for the film Angels of War. *What would Australians or Americans think about this scene? What would a Papua New Guinea audience think about it?*

Fig. 32. New Guineans carrying a wounded soldier during the Second World War. What message is the photographer trying to get across to the reader?

- **c** How many American troops were on Funafuti Atoll at the peak of the occupation?
- **d** Why did the Australian and Japanese military execute Bougainvillians?
- **e** During the war what was the item particularly missed on the Kiribati atolls?
- **f** How many Islanders died during the fighting on the Tolai Peninsula?
- **g** What caused the death of the two Islanders killed on Funafuti Atoll during the war?
- **h** How many Papua New Guineans were conscripted into the Labour Corps?
- **i** What was the impact of disease on the local population during the war years? Why was this a problem only associated with the war?

2 Draw a sketch map showing the Japanese expansion through the war.

3 People who can remember the war years of 1942–1945 are the older members of the community in the 1990s. Talk to these people about the impact of this period on their lives. What are their memories of the Pacific campaign?

4 The film, *Angels of War*, was promoted by the poster in Fig. 31. Do you think this is a just view of the impact of the war on the people concerned? Design a poster which portrays the reality of what happened to the people of Papua New Guinea.

'For enduring all of this'

Many Papuans were humiliated after the war when Australian officials confiscated the money and presents the villagers had earned selling artefacts. On Funafuti Atoll the Americans had planned to pay labour wages of seventy dollars a month, but British officials forced the Americans to pay only the normal pre-war wages of seven dollars and fifty cents a month. In the Solomon Islands it was widely believed that British officials kept the difference between what they saw as the generous offerings of the Americans and the two dollars a month they received as wages in the Labour Corps. The labourers complained. 'We were willing to die . . . we should get something because of the risk, don't spoil things for us. You whitemen (British) never go away empty handed . . .' After the war Wamanari, of the Sepik region in Papua New Guinea, spoke to a documentary film team and recalled that:

> The Australian government said, you work and later you'll be like us. But it hasn't happened. They said, you work for us and then we'll sit down at the same table and eat the same food with the same spoon . . . when the war finished in 1945 the Australian soldiers went home and got pensions and they're well off now. But me, I worked hard for nothing.

After the war Islanders began to question why their former 'masters' should come back and re-establish the old colonial regimes. Although some American soldiers advised Solomon Islanders to negotiate with the British for a better deal, the labourers and those who stayed in the villages lacked strong leaders who could argue and negotiate on an equal level with English-speaking officials and planters.

On Malaita Island in the Solomon Islands, which had a longer history of contact with traders and plantation work, dissatisfaction led to a major political movement, known first as the Native Council Movement or Native Union Council. By 1946 and 1947 the Maasina Rule Movement, as it became known, was able to arrange protest meetings of 5000 to 7000 people. It set up a local network controlled by Solomon Islanders in opposition to the British administration, and published orders, public notices and petitions:

> Order of Timothy George
>
> Roone
Sunday
24 Feb. 1946.
>
> I have ordered Figui Kalabeti, Junior Chief of Talitoo, Ataa District for to hold a meeting with you all the leading men of Ataa to help him choose out from among the people of Ataa villages and also from those of the other Founau. Tabitoo, Fanene, Sunaina, Asinawane people who have joined in with us in this movement of the 'Native Council Meeting' which is also called the Mercy Rule, some to sit for our council.
>
> We shall need for our house certain men for this purpose.
Firstly a council Headman:–Figui Kalabeti
Secondly a clerk
Thirdly two justices
Fourthly two groups of delegates
Fifthly say two lots of chiefs, one lot for each group of delegates.

Please take care to choose out
a. men whom we can trust
b. men of good report
c. humble and sensible men
d. men who will stand for the 'Right'.
This is my order,

From Timothy George.

It was gradually weakened by the colonial government and lost its support in the villages. The Solomons eventually gained full independence in 1978.

In Kiribati protest marches were organised late in 1944, asking America to take over and rule and petitions were forwarded through the village High Chiefs indicating that the people did not want the British to return. The British did return and, after the last Americans left in 1946, they ordered that the former airstrips be replanted in coconuts. It was clear to the people of Kiribati that the British did not want them to have contact with the outside world.

Many Islanders felt doubly betrayed. Their 'masters' had fled leaving them to an unknown fate. Then they came back and denied them the fruits of the victory. The friendliness and sharing of the Japanese and the Americans had impressed villagers who had always been treated as 'second class'. They had also seen black people (American negro soldiers) sharing church services, food and entertainment and being treated equally with white men. They had seen more of Western technology, material possessions and wealth than ever before. Many wondered when they would get their fair share of this wealth.

Today many Islanders must wonder why they never see themselves in the thousands of war movies, books and comics about the war. In a typical example, a book of 323 pages on the Pacific war by the popular American war historian Edwin Hoyt, has only one line which mentions the people of the Pacific. Hoyt notes that 'friendly islanders promised . . . they would bury the American dead'. Hoyt adds in a bracket, 'and they did'.

It has taken a long time for recognition to be given to the contribution of Islanders in the war. It was not until 1980 that the first payments to war veterans were made by the Papua New Guinea government.

The war changed the relationship between Europeans and Islanders. The Europeans' unchallenged position as 'master' had been questioned. Judith Bennett, an historian writing about the Solomon Islands, suggests that 'the status of the Europeans would never be quite the same again. The war brought about a loss of face for the whites . . .' In the history which they have written, the people of Tuvalu record the war in this way:

> . . . since it changed the world within which Tuvalu had to live, the impact of the war was profound. For it helped put an end to the age of colonial rule, and brought into being a world in which colonies were to be prepared for independent nationhood.

The war was also a very dramatic, tragic and trying personal experience involving family breakup, death, deprivation and psychological stress. Wanamari, of the Sepik region, bitterly noted that 'for enduring all of this, we have got nothing'.

A CTIVITIES

1 In response to question 2 (see p. 53) you made a list of ten options. Add or delete others that you now consider were options. Rank the final list from those least likely to those most likely to have occurred.

2 Check the message you wrote in answer to question 3 (see p. 53). Rewrite that message adding or deleting information you now consider important.

3 Write answers to these questions giving your own opinion.

- **a** In villages located **between** the combat zones, what do you think the major impact of the war might have been?
- **b** In villages **within** the occupation or perimeter zone of one of the forces, what do you think the major impact of the war might have been?
- **c** Why did it take another thirty or forty years for islands affected by the war to get their full independence?
- **d** Why did Islanders like the Americans more than than their former British and Australian rulers?
- **e** If you had been involved in the war as a supply depot organiser, what rules would you have established for relations between soldiers and local villagers? List these guidelines or rules.
- **f** What is your opinion on the issue of paying island labourers a European wage rate for war work, rather than the lower, pre-war 'native' rate?

R ESEARCH PROJECTS

1 On a map of the Pacific, colour in the Pacific Islands occupied by Japan, Australia and the United States between 1942 and 1945.

2 Watch the film *Angels of War*.

3 Read the novel *The Crocodile* by Papuan writer Vincent Eri (Penguin 1973).

4 Interview a former soldier from the Papua New Guinea campaigns. What can he remember about the invasion?

5 Listen to the ABC tapes of *Taim Bilong Masta* by Hank Nelson (Part 22 was on the war) or read the book of the same name.

Resources

Alaima, T. et al. *Kiribati: Aspects of History*, Ch. 9, USP/Institute for Pacific Studies, Suva, 1979.

Angels of War, Ronin Films, Canberra, 16 mm film.

Bennett, J. *Wealth of the Solomons*, Ch. 13, University of Hawaii Press, Honolulu, 1987.

Howard, C. *Mariquita: A Tragedy of Guam*, USP/Institute for Pacific Studies, Suva, 1986.

Laracy, H. & White, G. (eds) 'Taim bilong faet: World War II in Melanesia', *O'O': A Journal of Solomon Islands Studies*, Solomon Islands University Extension Centre, Honiara.

Laracy, H. (ed.) *Tuvalu: A History*, Ch. 18, USP/Institute for Pacific Studies, Suva, 1983.

Oliver, D. *Bougainville: A Personal History*, Ch. 7, Melbourne University Press, 1973.

Robinson, N. *Villagers at War: Some Papua New Guinean Experiences in World War II*, ANU Press, Canberra, 1979.

7

Retracing the Past: the Voyage of the 'Hokule'a'

Focus question

Can 20th century canoe reconstructions accurately repeat voyages made in ancient times?

To Tahiti and back

In 1974 it was announced that a 10 000 kilometre voyage to and from Hawaii to Tahiti would take place. The special canoe being built was the *Hokule'a*, a double-hulled canoe similar to those constructed by ancient Hawaiians, perhaps a thousand or more years ago.

In May that year a headline in *Pacific Islands Monthly*, a Pacific news magazine, announced that 'Hawaiians will sail back into history'. The organisers hoped that Hawaiian people would become enthusiastic about their own history. The organisers also hoped to prove that ancient navigators could find their way to and from Tahiti, that men and women and children could survive such long voyages, and that the construction and navigating skills of both canoes and people could be revived. In 1976 the voyage to Tahiti and back took place and enormous interest was shown by both Hawaiians and Tahitians in the style, capability and legendary past of voyaging canoes. But just three months later *Pacific Islands Monthly* ran another headline: '*Hokule'a* does it but it wasn't pure Polynesian say critics'. The debate continued for several years but the *Hokule'a* voyage has been generally recognised as a turning point in the modern day history of the Hawaiian people.

For many Hawaiian and part-Hawaiian people the voyage was at last proof of the original long distance voyages made by their prehistoric ancestors. If the *Hokule'a* could sail to and from Tahiti, they argued, it was possible that Polynesians from Tahiti's neighbouring islands of Raiatea or the Marquesas had indeed first explored and settled in Hawaii in the 6th Century AD. But in the wake of the *Hokule'a*, there were also cries of anger.

Accusations were made that the voyage was a fake because the canoe was not a true reconstruction of a prehistoric Hawaiian voyaging canoe. Critics of the voyage claimed that a canoe constructed in 1974, relying on legends and myths for the design, materials, construction techniques, food and equipment could not

Ethnic composition of Hawaii, 1974
(Estimated population of Hawaii in 1974 was about 800 000)

	%
American-born/European parents	27
Japanese	26
Hawaiian/part-Hawaiian	17
Filipino	10
Mixed race	10
Chinese	4
Korean	1
Negro	1
all others	4

(Note: 25% of all people are children of mixed marriages)

Fig. 33. Following the stars. Why does the route bend towards the east? Would it be similar to the path of the original long-distance voyages made by their ancestors?

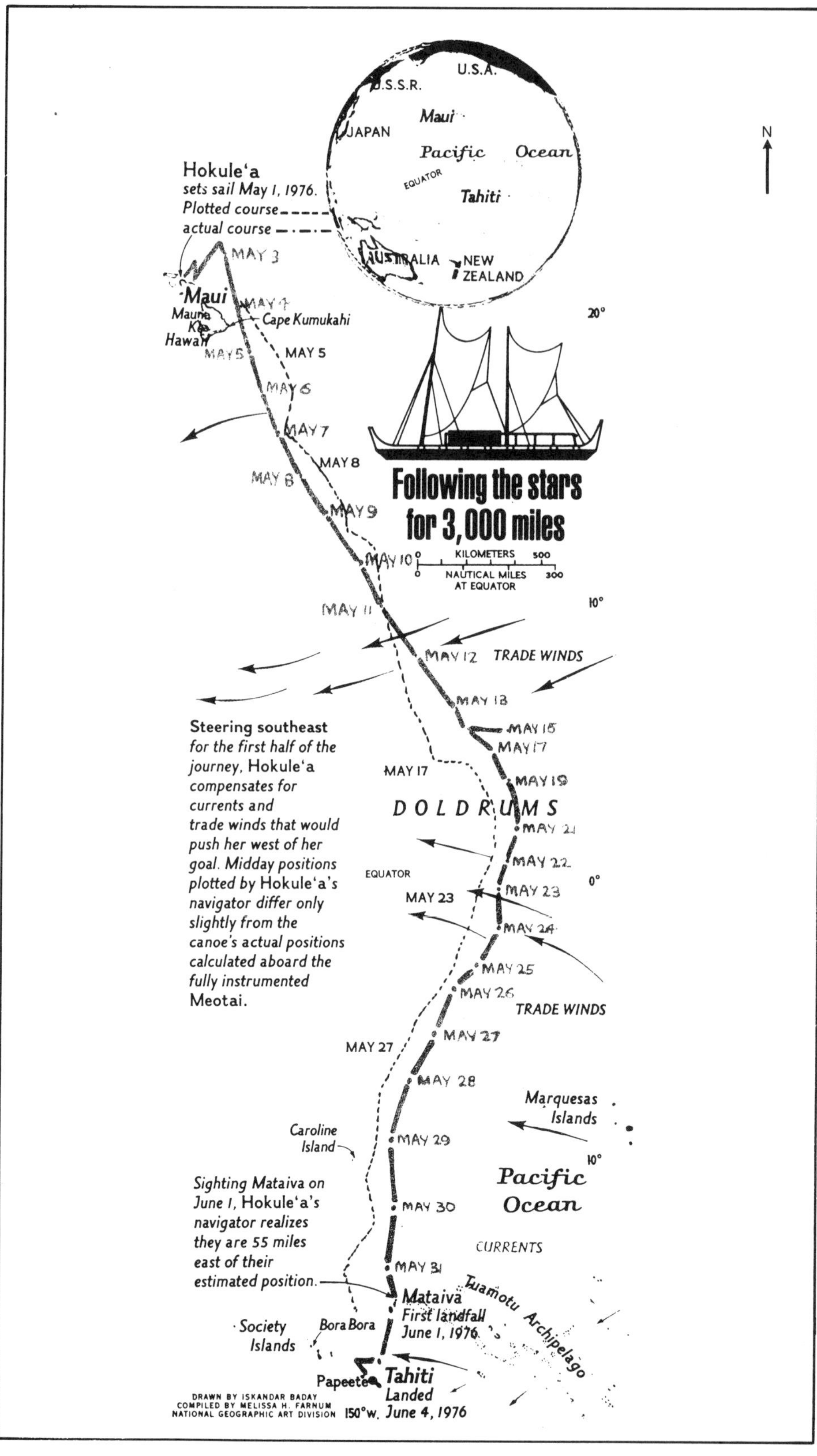

Hokule'a, the canoe, taught modern man an old lesson

Hawaiians will sail back into history

HOKULE'A DOES IT BUT 'IT WASN'T PURE POLYNESIAN' SAY CRITICS

WHAT THE HOKULE'A'S VOYAGE WAS ALL ABOUT

In Hokule'a's wake — and it'll be pure Polynesian!

Fig. 34. Is there a difference between a replica and a reconstruction? What are the differences between a 'pure' Hawaiian voyage and another voyage?

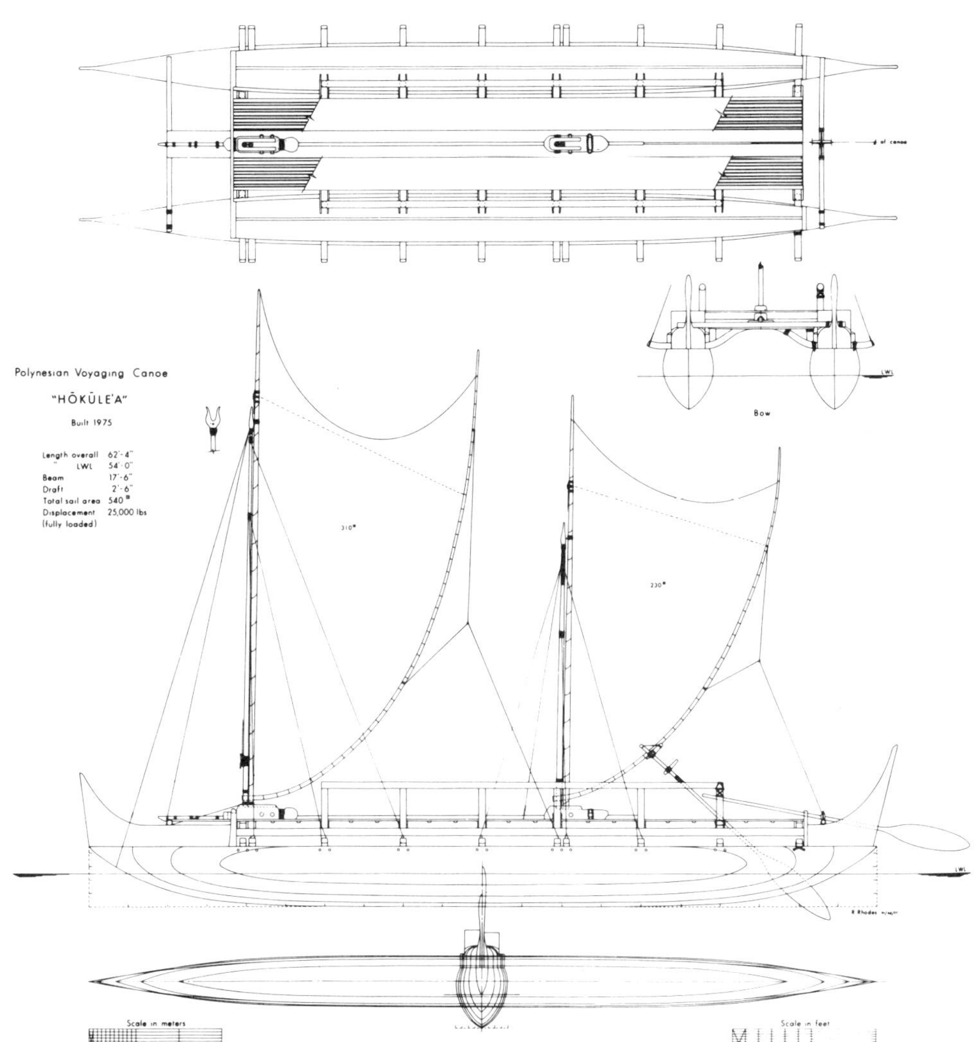

Fig. 35. Plan of the Hokule'a. *List the visible differences between a modern catamaran and the* Hokule'a. *How long was a Viking long-ship? How long was James Cook's* HMS Endeavour? *How were sails arranged on a Viking long-ship?*

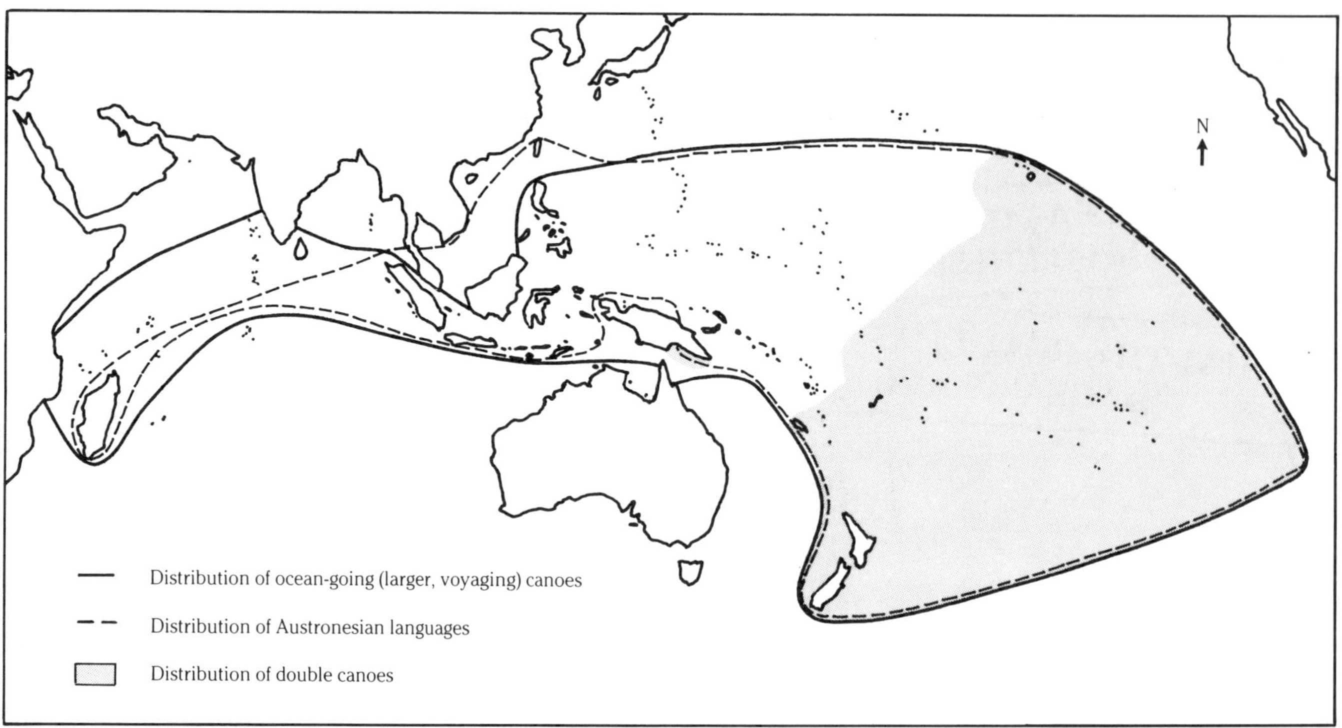

Fig. 36. In what way does the map suggest an ancient common culture for people within this distribution area? Why aren't ancient Aboriginal Australians included in this zone? Why did double canoes only develop in the eastern region?

be considered 'pure' Polynesian. They argued that if even the smallest item in the construction: materials, food or navigation, used in the voyage came from the 20th century, then the voyage was a 'fake'.

The problem of historical accuracy is around us everywhere today — in films, in television mini-series and particularly during anniversaries and bicentennial celebrations and re-enactments. Today there are many 'authentic' villages, museums and historical parks and many 'traditional' dance companies, craft centres and cultural groups. Each one claims to show how it really was in the past. The *Hokule'a* was an attempt to show how Polynesian navigators crossed a vast ocean to settle in Hawaii. Was it a fake? What did it prove?

In May–June 1976 the *Hokule'a* made the 10 000 kilometre crossing from Hawaii to Papeete on the island of Tahiti. A month later it turned around and sailed back to Hawaii.

▲▲▲ Related questions ▲▲▲

1 Where did the first Hawaiians come from?

2 What were the aims of the *Hokule'a* voyage?

3 How did Hawaiians respond to the voyage?

4 What did other Polynesians and Pacific Islanders think about the Hawaii–Tahiti voyage?

5 What skills did prehistoric navigators rely upon for accuracy and success?

ACTIVITIES

1 If accurate knowledge of ancient canoes has been nearly all lost, what aspects of modern technology can be permitted before a reconstruction voyage is considered a fake? List five 'modern' items that you would accept before you would reject a voyage of this nature?

2 In a modern-day reconstruction voyage, how important is it that historical accuracy be enforced?

3 Copy the map of the route of the *Hokule'a* from Hawaii to Tahiti. (See Fig. 33) Use a large piece of paper (at least A3 size or bigger). Mark only:
- ▲ the equator
- ▲ North
- ▲ the main island groups — Hawaii, Marquesas, Tuamotu, and Society Islands (A few dots will do for the islands, but note their position as accurately as possible.)
- ▲ the estimated and actual courses

Fig. 37. This is a sketch of an out-rigger canoe. Who would 'own' such a canoe? Was it dug out from a single tree? How many days or hours of labour would it take to build a canoe like this?

Out-riggers and double hulls

Long-distance voyaging is one of the most exciting features of the history of the Pacific. Great voyages were common across much of the Pacific for trading and warfare. For example, in the year 1880, the trader Richard Parkinson recorded that no fewer than sixteen large canoes arrived at Ontong Java, the northernmost tip of the Solomon Islands, after having crossed a thousand or more kilometres of open ocean. In 1916 a British sailing ship took nine days to tack back and forward against wind and currents between the atolls of Abemama and Kuria, only to find on the morning it reached Kuria that nine large baurua (deep-water out-rigger canoes) had arrived as well, having made the same crossing overnight. In the 1930s and 1940s there were still baurua in Kiribati, some more than 30 metres long and capable of carrying over a hundred people.

These large voyaging canoes disappeared from much of the Pacific between 1900 and 1940, replaced by square-rigged ships, or European-manufactured steam and propellor driven ships and smaller craft. After the Second World War the aluminium runabout and the outboard motor completed the gradual process in which large canoes disappeared.

But ancient voyaging and migration traditions lived on in family genealogies. Great myths and legends were told in dance, story-telling, music and singing. There were also non-Pacific Islander historians and anthropologists interested in researching and writing about the canoes, navigation and origins of the Polynesian people.

One of these was David Lewis, whose book *We the navigators* was a major step forward in recognising the sea-going skills of Polynesians. Another participant in the *Hokule'a* project was Ben Finney, who taught courses on the Pacific at the University of Hawaii and who had already built a small Hawaiian-style canoe before becoming involved in the Hawaii–Tahiti project.

Hawaiians, however, had lost most of the sail-making, canoe-building and food-making skills of their ancestors. They had become too westernised, too Americanised.

Fig. 38. A modern boat. Could this type of activity be included as part of a maritime tradition?

A performance-accurate voyage

There were several people in Hawaii with a desire to build large Hawaiian canoes. In 1974, Ben Finney (a haole or white man), Herb Kane (part-Hawaiian) and Tommy Holmes (also a haole, but born in Hawaii) got together and formed the Polynesian Voyaging Society. They set about raising $60 000 to finance the project and started thinking of ideas for sponsorships, advertising and community involvement. They argued about what the voyage was trying to prove. They argued about the length of the giant double-hulled canoe they would build and they argued about how it would be constructed. The original Hawaiian canoes they wanted to copy had been made from a single log with planks closely fitted to the sides to increase the height. But this idea was rejected, as Ben Finney explained:

> To try and revive the lost art in order to build a big voyaging canoe the likes of which had not been seen for hundreds of years would have been to invite disaster. So we had to pass up the opportunity to test the strength and durability of ancient materials . . .

They decided to copy the design of ancient canoes, and build it from modern materials.

They hoped to use the same woven sails, coconut fibre rope (called sennit), lashings, paddles and spars as those used by ancient voyagers. But the canoe was not an accurate replica; emphasis was placed on the voyage being performance-accurate.

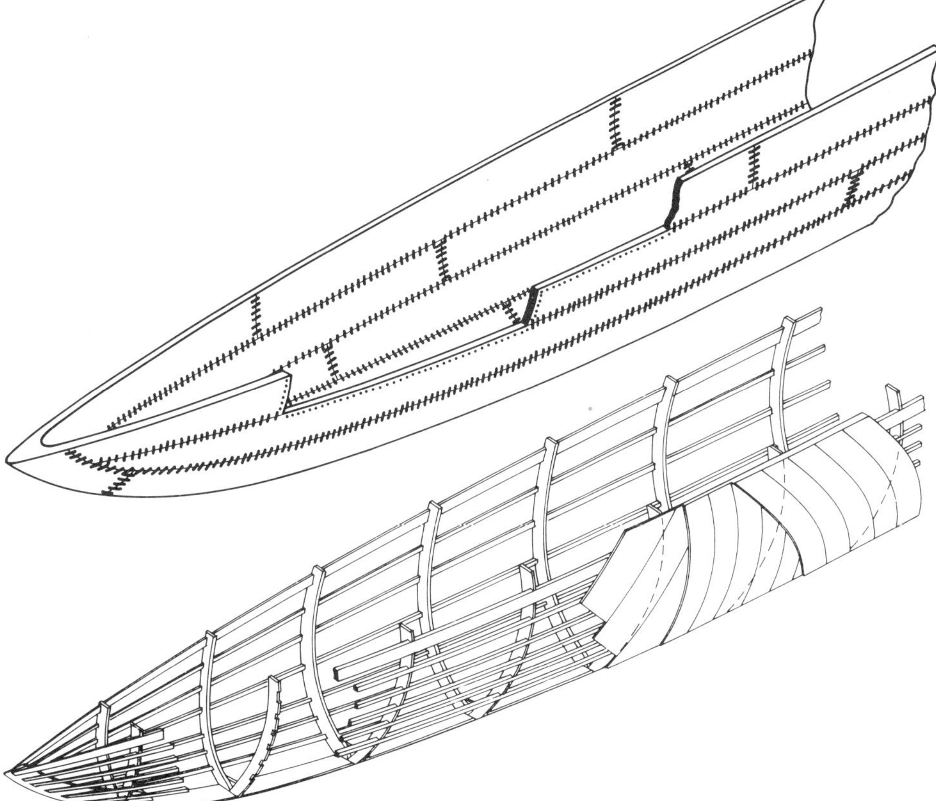

Fig. 39. Canoe construction: traditional and modern. What differences are there between the two?

Taboo, taboo, taboo

The *Hokule'a* was eventually launched with a solemn and moving traditional ceremony. Many Hawaiian-born people had become involved in the project and requests for places on the voyage to Tahiti were many times the number who could eventually sail. After the launching the *Hokule'a* went on trial trips around the Hawaiian Islands and everywhere it landed more solemn and traditional ceremonies took place. Many Hawaiians were noticed just sitting and staring at the canoe for hours. It was serving its purpose. It had sparked a cultural revival. Hawaiians began searching for and making traditional recipes for the coming voyage, and recalling long-forgotten chants and dances associated with voyaging.

There was also plenty of advice offered to the crew. Expert Hawaiian surfers, swimmers and paddlers were recommended and long arguments balanced the value of one man against another as paddler or 'waterman'. Although experts in the coastal waters around their own beaches and bays, few Hawaiians had deep-water voyaging or ocean-sailing experience. The trials around the islands gradually gave everyone the confidence to tackle the long trip to Tahiti.

Other advice, or taboo (bans), was more disturbing. As the *Hokule'a* took on the appearance of a Hawaiian cultural revival it was suggested that no haole should participate. Others declared that no women should ever go on board, or that carrying bananas on board would prevent fish from being caught (an essential part of the voyaging diet). Others declared that yellow and black colours should not be used. Some complained about the fibreglass and marine ply hull, and others that a safety yacht equipped with radio and radar should not accompany the *Hokule'a*.

As no Hawaiian could be found who could navigate using only the stars, wave patterns, the flight paths of birds and other natural signs, a respected navigator from Satawal in the Caroline Islands (in Micronesia) was invited to join the *Hokule'a* as sailing master. Along with another famous navigator from Satawal, he was perhaps the last in the Pacific who could navigate long distances using only the star-path methods of ancient voyagers.

A pig, dog, cock and hen were also chosen and many traditional plants and seeds were packaged for the voyage, just as they had been centuries before. Packages of dried bananas, dried fish and other traditional foods were also stowed aboard. Because Hawaiians had lost many of these skills, dried bananas were obtained from the Cook Islands and woven or plaited matting sails from the Caroline Islands. (On the voyage canvas was used instead of the traditional woven, matting sails and tinned food was used after only a few days of 'Polynesian' diet. They also used camping lanterns and had a modern yacht as a safety escort.)

To Tahiti and return

On May 1 1976 the *Hokule'a* left the island of Maui laden with supplies and a crew of seventeen men and headed south-east for Tahiti. They had three aims:

▲ to judge the efficiency of navigation by the stars (no modern equipment was used on the journey)

- ▲ to judge how well Polynesian plants and animals travelled on long-distance voyages
- ▲ to try out foods preserved in the traditional manner

On June 4 1976 the *Hokule'a* landed in Papeete to be met by 15 000 people, the biggest crowd ever seen in Tahiti. Many island communities had composed special songs of welcome and the beaches were packed with well-wishers. Several hundred boats and small outrigger canoes rushed to meet the *Hokule'a*. David Lewis, one of those on board, wrote that 'None of us could ever forget that welcome. It was clear that the voyage of the *Hokule'a* had tapped deep well-springs of Polynesian identity'.

An organisation in Tahiti, called the Tainui Association had been formed to welcome the *Hokule'a* voyagers and to organise feasts, speeches and visits to villages on Tahiti. The Tainui Association also planned to use the visit of the *Hokule'a* to stimulate interest in the building of a voyaging canoe in Tahiti.

Tahitians are also Polynesians. The Tahitians knew that Polynesians in Hawaii had become 'Americanised' through mixed-race marriages and the impact of American education, television, employment, business and sport. Tainui Association members were worried about the similar influence of French government and education in Tahiti. At the time of the *Hokule'a*'s arrival, some Tahitians were campaigning for a reduction in French influence in Tahiti. A Tainui leader told Ben Finney that:

> . . . we saw the sails of *Hokule'a* on the horizon. That gave us courage. That made us think with pride of ourselves as Polynesians and gave us strength to persist . . .

On July 4 1976 the *Hokule'a* left Tahiti. Five thousand kilometres of open ocean and twenty-three days later she sailed into Honolulu Harbour to another huge cheering crowd.

Hokule'a is a hoax

The voyage was a fake, some claimed, because of the fibreglass, the haole crew members, the use of nails, nylon and canvas, and protective waterproof clothing. There were accusations that a secret compass and a cassette recording with navigating directions was used. For many Hawaiians the major complaint was that they assumed the *Hokule'a* was Hawaiian-built, Hawaiian-sailed and a purely Hawaiian venture. For them it was a disappointment that the voyage had haole equipment, some haole crew and haole leaders. Others, however, saw the voyage as a major break-through in the revival of Polynesian culture. Looking back on the voyage, David Lewis's opinion was:

> The effects of the *Hokule'a*'s achievement spread through the islands like ripples from a stone tossed in a pond. Soon after, new voyaging canoes came under construction in Tahiti and Hawaii; the Islanders are beginning to rediscover the dignity of their voyaging heritage.

Ben Finney claimed that the possibility of deliberate long-distance voyaging by Polynesian navigators had been proven. It had also proved that double-hulled canoes could make long voyages into the wind and that non-instrument navigation could be relied upon for accuracy over thousands of kilometres of ocean.

The pig, chickens and dog thrived and survived the trip. The seeds and plants were transplanted in Tahiti and only the food experiment had failed. A young Fijian, studying in Hawaii at the time, wrote:

> *Hokule'a* has shown the rest of the world a part of its past . . . *Hokule'a* has been an outstanding success . . . The *Hokule'a* has re-kindled an awareness in the people of Hawaii of the richness of their heritage.

In March 1978 the *Hokule'a* set off again for Tahiti but capsized in heavy seas shortly after leaving Hawaii. After being salvaged, relashing and some minor redesigning were completed. In April 1980 the *Hokule'a* again successfully crossed to Tahiti.

The captain for the voyage in 1980 was an Hawaiian who had sailed on the original return voyage from Tahiti to Hawaii in 1976. The voyage was a giant step back in time, he said. 'During the day the crew used ocean currents, sea swells and the flight patterns of birds to steer the canoe towards Tahiti. At night the stars were our guide.' Once again the *Hokule'a* had passed the test of ancient navigational skills and human endurance.

ACTIVITIES

1. Which islands is it suggested that the original Hawaiians came from?
2. Describe the ethnographic distribution of Oceanic-speaking populations shown in Fig. 36.
3. Why were out-rigger canoes designed for this region? Build a model of an out-rigger canoe and conduct a trial of its suitability to withstand strong winds and heavy rain. After testing, remove the out-rigger and conduct the same tests. How did the stability of the craft change? What impact did this piece of technology have on the ability of the people to move around the Pacific?
4. What is a baurua?
5. What is sennit?
6. In your own words describe the meaning of the phrase 'a performance-accurate voyage'.
7. What materials were used to make the hull of the *Hokule'a*?
8. What were the two organisations formed in Hawaii and Tahiti to assist the *Hokule'a* project?

9 How many people were estimated to have welcomed the *Hokule'a* in Papeete when she arrived?

10 List six complaints or criticisms of the *Hokule'a* voyage.

Taratai, Mo'olele, Binabina, and Maharek Maihar

The *Hokule'a* was an important step for Hawaiians trying to recapture their traditions. The *Hokule'a* served its purpose by making two voyages to Tahiti and one to Samoa. Since then it has become a floating classroom where Hawaiians learn the art and skills of navigation and voyaging.

On other islands a similar revival is underway. As large canoes have not been seen for many generations and the skills of the past have been ignored, attempts are being made to revive the ancient voyaging skills of the ancestors. On some islands these skills have been fortunately retained by a few respected individuals and communities.

In Micronesia, for example, a canoe sailed 2800 kilometres from Satawal Atoll to Okinawa Island near Japan in December 1975, for an International Marine Expo. Although the trip had been made by 'hopping' from island to island, it was the longest deliberate voyage in recent Micronesian history.

In 1976, during the American Bicentennial 1776–1976, an 8 metre, inter-island, out-rigger sailing canoe, the *Maharek Maihar*, left Pulawat Atoll in the Truk Islands. It reached Guam on a planned voyage to the United States. Arrangements for the long voyage then fell through and it was later stranded on Saipan Island. (A new project plans to restore the out-rigger for display on Saipan.)

In 1976 a voyage similar to the *Hokule'a* took place in Kiribati. A great voyaging canoe or baurua was constructed on Tarawa Atoll and sailed, using modern navigation techniques, on a 2500 kilometre course south to Fiji. The *Taratai* reached its destination and the New Zealander who led the project was pleased that they had 'proved beyond doubt that Pacific Islanders had the capacity to sail across the sea, easily and confidently'.

The *Taratai* had been constructed using traditional building materials and techniques, but was not an exact reconstruction. It was merely a small canoe design enlarged to look like the ancient baurua of the past. After the Fiji voyage the *Taratai* was cargo-freighted to New Zealand and is now on display in the National Museum Canoe Collection in Wellington.

In the Hawaiian Islands, even before the *Hokule'a* left, Islanders on Maui Island had constructed a large double-hulled paddling canoe, the *Mo'olele* or 'Flying Lizard'. Ancient ceremonies for the launching of canoes and the welcoming of canoes from other islands were revived and interest among Hawaiians increased.

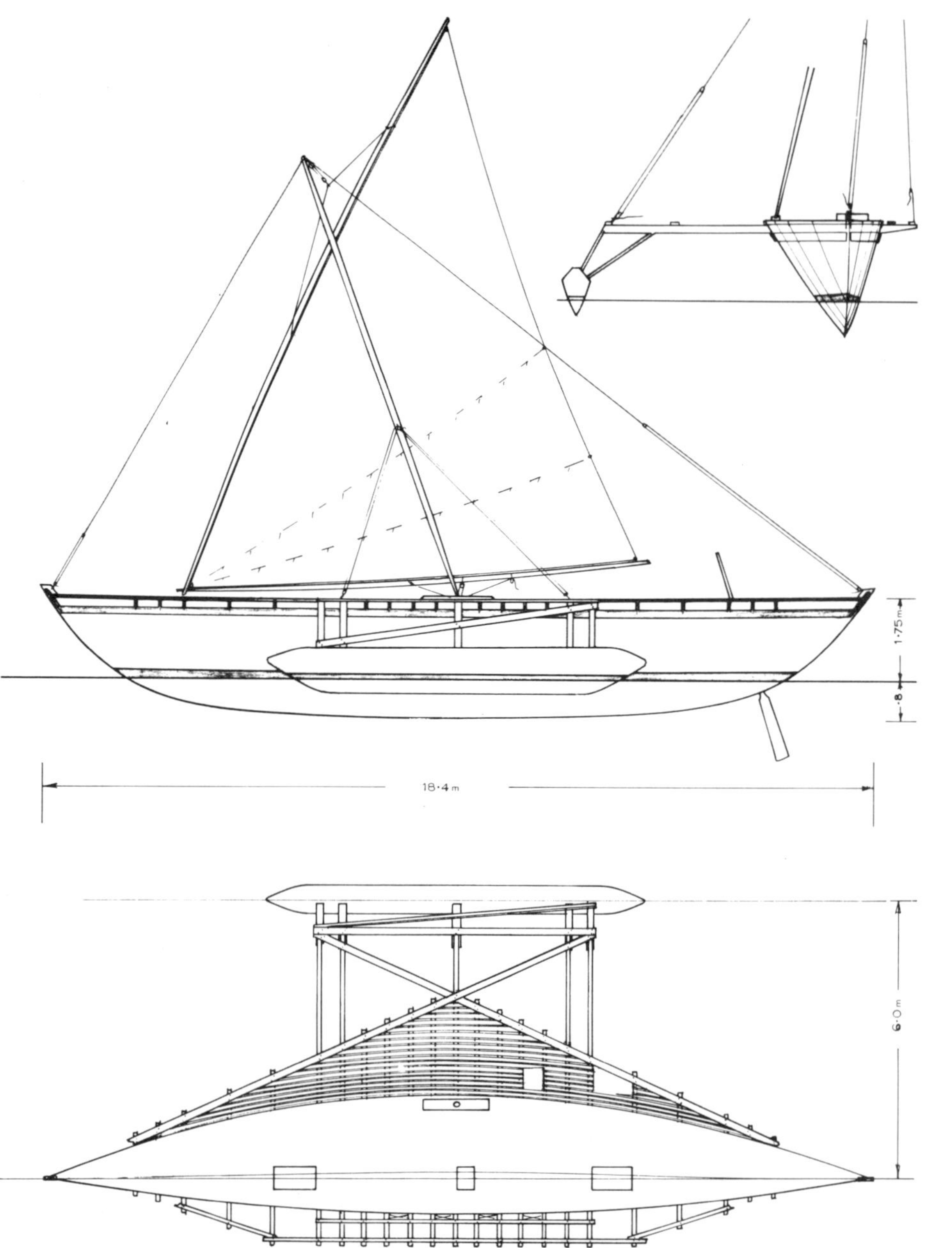

Fig. 40. The Taratai. *What are the differences between the* Taratai *and the* Hokule'a*?*

On Gela Island in the Solomon Islands a war canoe, of a type not seen for many generations, was constructed in 1980–1981. The *Binabina* was the largest type of canoe made by the Gela people and had been used for war or for carrying chiefs and leaders on special ceremonial trips. It was a single-hull paddling canoe made by planking the sides rather than by hollowing out a single tree trunk. Although it was built for speed, it could withstand heavy weather and was big enough for warriors to wield shields and clubs should an attack take place at sea.

The *Binabina* was built in June 1981 at Haroro village, the last place in the Solomon Islands where people had retained the knowledge and skills to con-

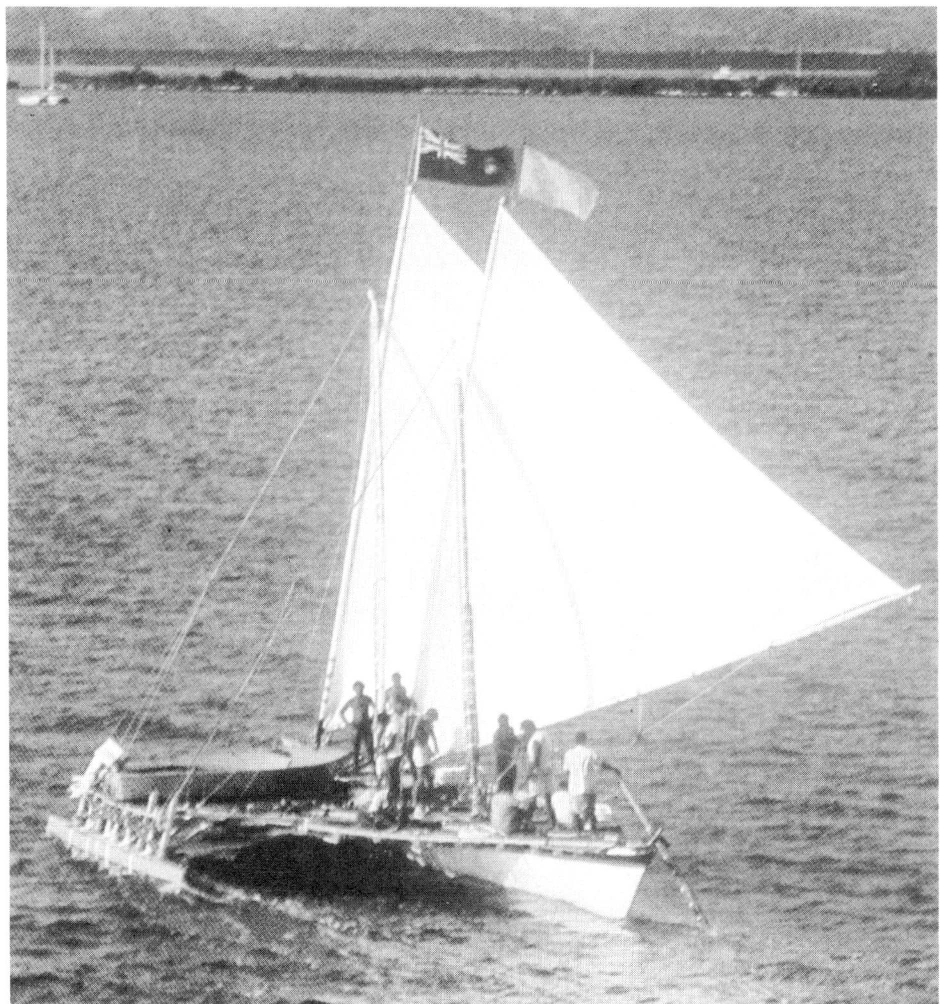

Fig. 41. The Taratai *is now on display in the National Museum Canoe Collection in Wellington, New Zealand.*

struct such a canoe. The *Binabina* made a two-day passage from Gela Island to Guadalcanal. Robert Pule, one of the *Binabina* organisers, in his arrival speech said that:

> . . . an important part of our tradition has come back with a loud noise to take its proper place. It is a good thing to learn, to wake and to try and foster the knowledge of our origins and to educate the young people in the true customs and traditions of their ancestors.

There have been many similar voyages and reconstruction projects across the Pacific and in other parts of the world.

In another ocean, the Indian Ocean, in 1983 an attempt was made to prove that people known as the Austronesian language speakers had voyaged from South-east Asia to Africa and back. Some historians and archaeologists suggested this voyaging occurred in pre-historic times, so a replica canoe, the *Sarimanok*, was built for a voyage across the Indian Ocean from the Philippines to Madagascar.

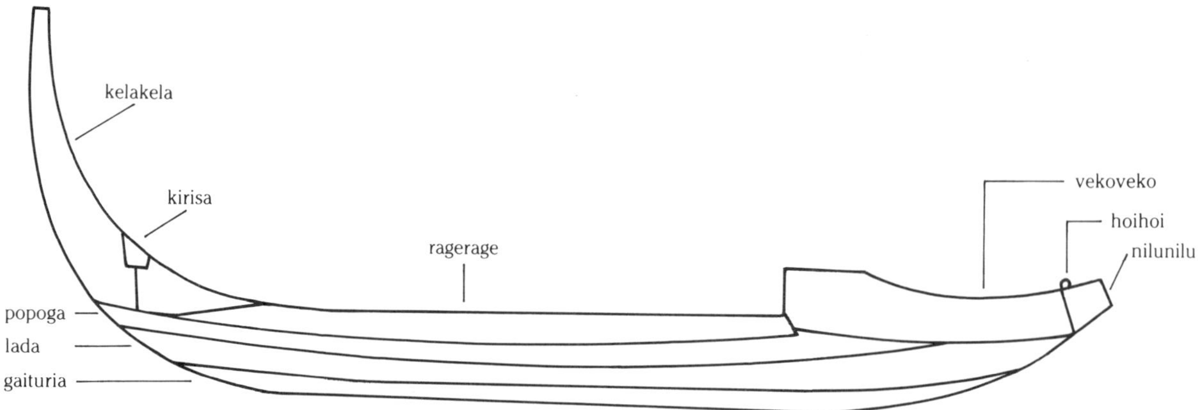

Fig. 42. The main sections of the Binabina.

Hundreds of years had passed since the last large Austronesian style canoe was built so the builders of the *Sarimanok* undertook a long search for information about ancient canoe design and construction. They found details in a variety of places:

- ▲ in archaeological digs in the Philippines and Malaysia (from the 3rd and 7th centuries)
- ▲ in carved pictures on the stone walls of 9th century Buddhist temples in Java in Indonesia
- ▲ in drawings and etchings of European explorers in the 16th century who had visited the Philippines and Indonesia

The art on the walls of caves, legends, some early drawings by European explorers, and construction skills handed down over the centuries enabled the *Sarimanok* to be built. In Tahiti and Hawaii, when the *Hokule'a* was being built, there was similar evidence of large double-hulled canoes. In Hawaii this research had enabled the Polynesian Voyaging Society to build the *Hokule'a*.

Not all replica voyages have had films or books produced about them in the same way as the *Hokule'a*, *Taratai* and *Binabina*. No doubt some have been 'fakes' or only partly accurate reconstructions, but in some way all have contributed to the revival of an ancient maritime heritage and created renewed interest in deep-sea, long-distance voyaging.

ACTIVITIES

1 Do the following map work.

a Complete the map (see question 3, p. 69), by adding short descriptions (in boxes or balloons) along each side of the route. These should inform a reader about various aspects of the voyage of the *Hokule'a*.

b Select a suitable main heading and add it to the map.

2 Check your answers to questions 1 and 2 on p. 69. Have you changed your mind? If so, change any of the answers you made at the beginning.

3 Now look at your answer to question 2 on p. 69. In one sentence of about fifteen words write your final opinion on the question of accuracy in reconstruction voyages.

4 Answer these questions giving your own opinion.

a Why do you think Hawaiians lost interest in their voyaging heritage?

b Do you believe that ancient Polynesians in 600 AD could have sailed across an open ocean from Tahiti to Hawaii without the help of modern navigation instruments? Support your answer by writing a paragraph of at least seven sentences.

c Why do you think there are some men from atolls in Micronesia who have retained their voyaging skills longer than the Hawaiians?

d Do you think haoles should have been allowed to sail in the *Hokule'a*?
- ▲ support your answer by writing a statement of your opinion in one sentence
- ▲ list three arguments (or pieces of evidence) in support of your opinion

e Using the complaints voiced against the *Hokule'a*, imagine you are a crew member and write and audio-tape, or present to the class, a speech defending the voyage.

RESEARCH PROJECTS

1 Research the voyage of the *Sarimanok*.

2 Search for a book on myths and legends from the Pacific. Are voyaging or navigation skills a part of these stories? Look at the Hawaiian legends about the first people to land in Hawaii.

3 Read Ben Finney's book *Hokule'a: The way to Tahiti.*

4 Research canoe designs in several different parts of the world such as Egypt, Indonesia and Brazil. Are there any similarities?

5 Sketch, draw or copy (by enlarging) some canoes on to a large chart showing the basic features of a traditional double-hulled voyaging canoe. This might be contrasted with a drawing of a typical out-rigger canoe.

6 Visit a local 'authentic' historical park or museum. See if you can spot the inaccuracies. Then ask yourself if they really matter.

Resources

Emory, K. P. 'The coming of the Polynesians', *National Geographic*, December, 1974.

Finney, B. R. *Hokule'a: The way to Tahiti*, Dodd Mead, New York, 1979.

Kane, H. 'A canoe helps Hawaii recapture her past', *National Geographic*, April, 1976.

Lewis, D. *From Maui to Cook: The Discovery and Settlement of the Pacific*, Doubleday, 1977, pp. 197–204.

Pule, R. T. *Binabina: The Making of a Gela War Canoe*, University of the South Pacific, 1983.

Siers, J. *Taratai: A Pacific Adventure*, Millwood Publishers, New Zealand, 1977.

Thomas, S. D. *The Last Navigator*, Century Hutchinson, New York, 1988.

Note that extra information is available from the following *Pacific Islands Monthly* magazines: May 1974, pp. 21–23; August 1976, pp. 8–10; November 1976, pp. 8–9; December 1976, pp. 37–38; May 1977, pp. 37–41; June 1980, pp. 91–92.

Land Rights: the Struggle for Banaba

8

Focus question

Why have Banabans struggled to regain control of Banaba?

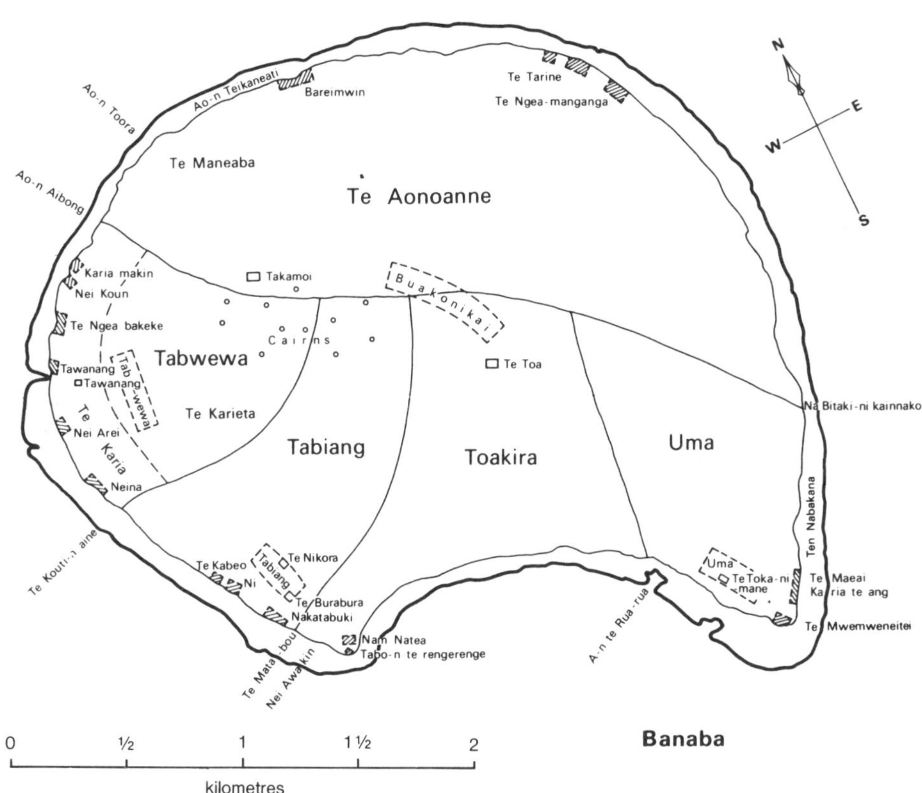

Fig. 43. Banaba. How are the size and position of boundaries determined? Are the boundaries on Banaba based on access to natural resources? What criteria would a mining company use to draw boundaries of its mining area?

A sense of outrage

Banaba (formerly Ocean Island) is situated half-way between Nauru and Kiribati. It is a small raised coral island about three kilometres long and two and a half kilometres wide. Between 1900 and 1940 it was mined extensively for phosphate (guano). During the Second World War the wells, forests, and gardens belonging to the Banaban people were destroyed by military fortifications and bombardments and the people evacuated by the Japanese. In 1945, when the war ended, they did not return to their small island in the central Pacific.

After being gathered from distant islands where they had been transferred during the war, the 1003 people (337 men, 297 women and 396 children) were made to move to an island purchased for them in Fiji by the British using money from mining royalties. They became the landholders and owners of Rabi Island, paid taxes to the Fijian government and became Fijian citizens. But they called themselves Banabans and Banaba was their home.

In the meantime the mining company, the British Phosphate Commission, returned to Banaba, imported hundreds of labourers from Kiribati and resumed the mining of phosphate. The island continued to be governed by the British as part of the Gilbert and Ellice Island Colony (GEIC). As well as paying for the right to use land, the mining company paid a percentage from the profits of mining (known as royalties) to Banaban people living in Fiji, and a larger percentage (up to 85 per cent) to the Gilbert and Ellice Island Colony government.

In 1916 Banaba had been included in the territory governed by the British colony, known as the Gilbert and Ellice Island Colony (made up of the Gilbert (Kiribati), Ellice, Phoenix and Line Islands). In 1979 the British left and the former colony split into two separate nations. The Ellice Islands became the separate nation of Tuvalu. The Gilbert Islands became Kiribati. Banaba was included in the new nation of Kiribati.

Banabans were upset for several reasons. They felt they were still the landholders or owners of the land on Banaba, even though they were now living in Fiji. They felt that since 1900, and particularly since 1945, they had not been given a fair share of royalties. They also felt that the Great Britain, Australia and New Zealand governments, the three partners in the British Phosphate Commission, had not compensated Banaban landholders for the destruction of their soil, gardens and trees. They also wanted Banaba to be independent rather than be included in Kiribati.

In their language the words Banaban and landholder are used interchangeably and given the same meaning. To be a Banaban meant being able to identify traditional family links with a specific plot of land, and to be a landholder. A person's land was their identity. The Banaban people saw the failure to recognise their rights as landholders as a denial that they existed.

Throughout the 20th century land rights and the problems which arise from land alienation have been a constant and bitter theme in the history of the people of the Pacific. Ownership struggles have involved neighbouring tribes or kin groups, invaders from afar, and European–Islander conflict. Land rights have become an area of tension as one group or another has tried to legally or illegally acquire land from existing landholders.

On Bougainville Island in Papua New Guinea, local landholders used violent tactics in the late 1980s to assert claims of land ownership and to seek proper payment of rents and royalties for use of their land for mining. In 1990 mining ceased on Bougainville and negotiations began between the Bougainvillians and the PNG government over Bougainville gaining status as a separate nation. In Hawaii, the exclusive use of beachfront property for tourist development has

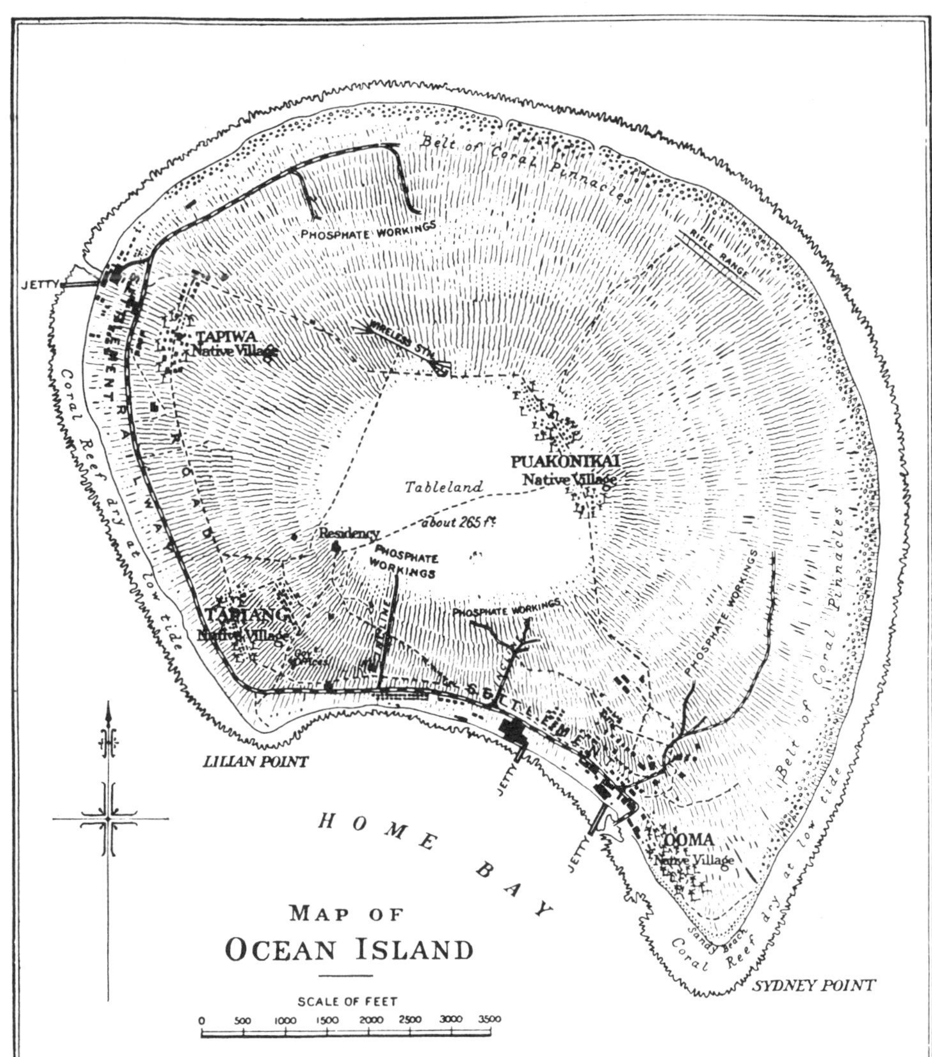

Fig. 44. A 1922 map of Banaba when it was known as Ocean Island. What features would Banabans today want to put on a map of their island?

been bitterly contested by Hawaiian-born protestors and others. In Fiji the question of Fiji-Indian land tenure (the right to use land) has long been a matter of dispute and surfaced again during the 1987 military coups. Maori land rights, fishing rights, payment of royalties and the legal tenure of large areas of land is a major area of conflict in New Zealand. In Australia, Aboriginal land rights are a long-running controversial political issue. In Tonga, land use and titles to land have caused bitter debate due to a shortage of land and the alleged 'unfair' practice of hereditary and absentee landholding.

The idea that land, identity and life are all the same is foreign to non-Pacific Islanders. But for the past two hundred years non-Pacific Islanders have signed land deals, contracts and sought to exchange titles for land. To their credit both colonial and newly independent governments have rigorously protected the land rights of the original inhabitants and very little land has been lost irrevocably.

However, to the Banabans, and to many other Pacific Islanders, the history of the 20th century is one of grief and despair over land they have lost and of which they now feel they are no longer a part.

▲▲▲ Related questions ▲▲▲

1 Why is ownership and the land so important to Pacific Islanders?

2 What does the phrase 'land rights' mean to Pacific Islanders?

3 What are the environmental effects of phosphate mining?

4 Why has Nauru gained independence while neighbouring Banaba has remained under British, and then Kiribati, control?

5 What was the link in the early 20th century between mining companies and colonial governments?

6 What precautions has Papua New Guinea taken to preserve land rights while allowing huge mining projects like Bougainville, Pogera and Ok Tedi to be developed?

7 What are the problems associated with the resettlement of Banaba?

8 What is the difference between surface rights, and under-surface rights to mine lands?

ACTIVITIES

1 On a map of the Pacific mark the following locations: Banaba, Nauru, Tarawa Atoll in Kiribati, and Rabi Island in Fiji.

2 Imagine you are the leaders of a Banaban negotiating team from Rabi Island about to meet with British Phosphate Company officials in 1975. What would be the ten demands you would present? List them.

3 Compare your list with another student's, then review your list and number the demands in importance from one to ten.

4 Who could the Banabans go to for help in regaining control of Banaba? List at least four possible people, institutions or organisations.

5 What long-term and short-term factors have affected Banaba in the 1990s? Give reasons for your answer.

6 Is there any similarity between the land rights battle in the Pacific Islands and that of the Aboriginals in Australia?

A most scandalous document

The Banaban people had lived and traded with Europeans for sixty years before phosphate mining began. The first Banaban–European contact occurred in 1801, when a Sydney vessel bound for China passed nearby. In the 1840s and 1850s there were whalers anchored at Banaba throughout the whaling season. A trader who visited Banaba in 1847 reported that there were seventeen beachcombers living there, though a year later another trader reported that there were then only seven. In the 1870s the Banaban population was halved when a serious drought caused many deaths, and others fled the island. In the 19th century as many as a thousand Banabans signed on as labour recruits to work in Hawaii, Queensland and Tahiti. In one day, in 1875, the brig *Flora* recruited sixty-five Banabans for Queensland sugar plantations. Missionaries first arrived in 1885.

Following the discovery, in 1900, that Banaba was an enormously rich and solid island of phosphate rock, the British Union Jack was raised and a mining company established a monopoly over mining. Banabans willingly traded food with the company officials, carried phosphate rock to storages near the beach and signed documents which gave the mining company the right to mine. There is no doubt that the Banabans did not understand what the Europeans meant by the signing of documents. The purchase of leases and the sale of land titles were alien concepts to them.

The main obstacles were the different languages and different meanings of words such as rights, tenure, lease, value and possession. The Banabans' link with the land remained absolute even if it was loaned, used or dug up by someone else. Europeans believed that land could be bought and sold permanently or that it was acceptable after mining to return it to the 'natives' stripped of trees, bare of surface soils, and looking rather like a jagged, desert landscape.

Fig. 45. Phosphate digging on Banaba. Can this landscape be used for any purpose? What does it need in order for it to be restored to a useable or arable condition?

The first mining licence in 1900 stated that the mining company would pay an annual rental of fifty English pounds ($A100) for twenty-one years. In 1902 this was changed to a 99-year period and the annual rental was replaced by a royalty of sixpence per ton. Individual landholders were also paid twenty English pounds per acre (an acre is 0.4 of a hectare).

In 1913 another 145 acres were acquired (at forty to sixty pounds per acre) and then a further 150 acres in 1931. Over the following years many negotiations took place over the royalties to be paid, and the hectares which could

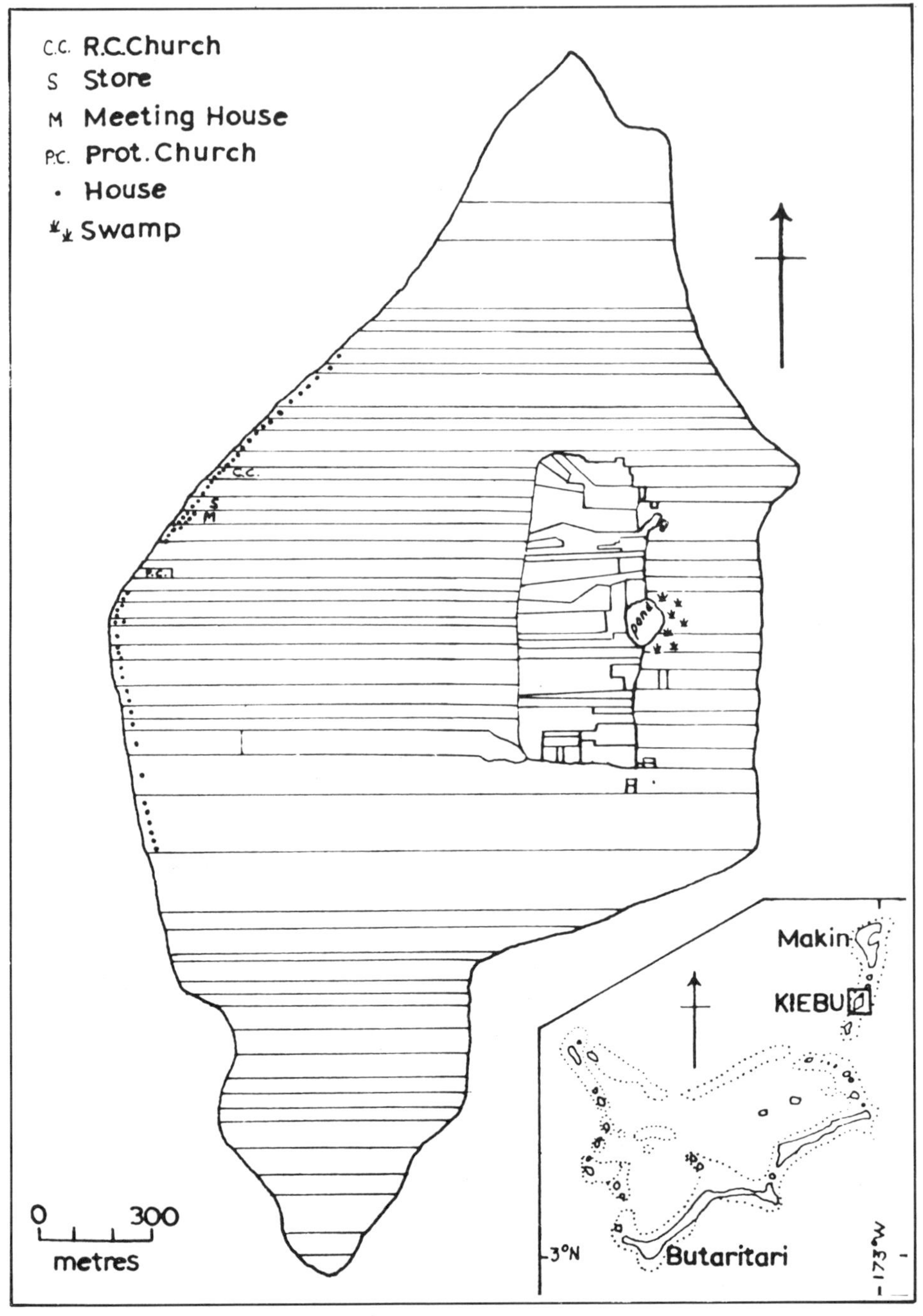

Fig. 46. Land division on Kiebu Atoll, Kiribati. As the plots are not of equal width or length, what criteria might be used to allocate plots? Why are the smaller fragmented plots situated in the eastern part of the atoll? If people do not live on their plot, how do they know who owns or uses each one?

be mined. By 1913, Banabans were expressing their dissatisfaction with their share of the mining profits, were worried about the amount of land being taken for mining, and were becoming concerned about the future of their lands when mining ceased. In 1920 the original Pacific Phosphate Company sold out to a partnership of three governments — Australia, New Zealand and Great Britain — and the British Phosphate Commission (BPC) took over mining. In a now famous letter sent in 1928 the British colonial official, Arthur Grimble, threatened the Banabans and demanded that they agree to the new mining deal being negotiated — much in the BPC's favour. Sir Arthur Grimble, once revered as a friend of the people, served in Kiribati and Banaba from 1914 to 1933. He was a land commissioner and then became the Colony's senior colonial official. His threatening letter to the Banabans did not become public until a court case in 1975.

To the people of Buakonikai,
Greetings,

You understand that the Resident Commissioner cannot again discuss with you at present as you have shamed his Important Chief, the Chief of the Empire, when he was fully aware of your views and your strong request to him and he had granted your request and restrained his anger and restored the old rate to you – yet you threw away and trampled upon his kindness.

The Chief has given up and so has his servant the Resident Commissioner because you have offended him by rejecting his kindnesses to you.

Because of this I am not writing to you in my capacity as Resident Commissioner but I will put my views as from your long-standing friend Mr Grimble who is truly your father, who has aggrieved you during this frightening day which is pressing upon you when you must choose *LIFE or DEATH.*

I will explain my above statement:

POINTS FOR LIFE

If you sign the agreement here is the life:

(1) Your offence in shaming the Important Chief will be forgiven and you will not be punished;

(2) The area of the land to be taken will be well known, that is only 150 acres, that will be part of the Agreement;

(3) The amount of money to be received will be properly understood and the Company will be bound to pay you, that will be part of the Agreement.

POINTS FOR DEATH

If you do not sign the Agreement:

(1) Do you think that your lands will not go? Do not be blind. *Your land will be compulsorily acquired for the Empire.*

If there is no Agreement who then will know the area of the lands to be taken?

If there is no Agreement where will the mining stop?

If there is no Agreement what lands will remain unmined?

Fig. 47. Arthur Grimble's letter. Today we can identify several crucial errors in this agreement. Is this agreement of any use in a legal battle over the ownership of Banaba today?

I tell you the truth – if there is no Agreement the limits of the compulsorily acquired lands on Ocean Island will not be known.

(2) And your land will be compulsorily acquired *at any old price*. How many pence per ton? I do not know. It will not be $10\frac{1}{2}$d. Far from it. How many pounds per acre? I do not know. It will not be £150. Far from it.

What price will be paid for coconut trees cut down outside the area?

I know well that it will remain at only £1.

Mining will be indiscriminate on your lands and the money you receive will be also indiscriminate. And what will happen to your children and your grandchildren if your lands are chopped up by mining and you have no money in the Bank?

Therefore because of my great sympathy for you I ask you to consider what I have said now that the day has come when you must choose LIFE or DEATH. There is nothing more to say. If you choose suicide then I am very sorry for you but what more can I do for you as I have done all I can.

I am, your loving friend and father,

Arthur Grimble.

P.S. You will be called to the signing of the Agreement by the Resident Commissioner on Tuesday next, the 7th August and if everyone signs the Agreement, the Banabans will not be punished for shaming the Important Chief and their serious misconduct will be forgiven. If the Agreement is not signed consideration will be given to punishing the Banabans. And the destruction of Buakonikai Village must also be considered to make room for mining if there is no Agreement.

After 1931 all Banabans received payments called annuities. The price per acre for individual landholders and rental payments was increased. Further payments were made by the company direct to a trust fund, to a provident fund, and to the Gilbert and Ellice Island Colony government. While this seemed an impressive pay-out, far more was going to the Gilbert and Ellice Island government (a British colony) than to the Banaban people. It was from these trust funds and provident funds that Rabi Island in Fiji was purchased in 1942 as a place to resettle Banabans. By then the company was arguing that for people following a customary village lifestyle, the destruction caused by the war had made Banaba uninhabitable. In 1947 a further deal between BPC, the Gilbert and Ellice Island Colony and the Banabans was negotiated. This deal later became a central issue in the now legendary 1972–75 court case.

By 1970 the Banabans on Rabi were seeking legal advice and had attracted media attention to their claim for compensation, for back payment of fairer royalties, and for Banaban independence from the Gilbert and Ellice Island Colony. When discussions began for the separation of the Gilbert and Ellice Islands in the 1970s, Banaban concern increased when it was found that Banaba was going to become part of the new nation of Kiribati.

With the help of the Fijian Prime Minister, the Banabans convinced Great Britain to postpone Gilbert and Ellice independence for two months until the Banaban question could be resolved. No solution was found and in 1979 Banaba became part of Kiribati. By this time the phosphate mine was running out. Some Banabans had been back to Banaba as phosphate workers, and some had squatted on the island to draw attention to their claims.

While all this was going on a major international event was unfolding. The people of Banaba took the nation of Great Britain to the courts of law to try and achieve a just level of compensation ($A11 million for replanting) and royalty payments ($A38 million 'wrongly' paid to the GEIC). After three years, then the longest trial in British legal history, the judge decided against the Banabans' claim. However, they gained a moral victory. They were not awarded compensation, but the judge advised the three governments that they should, as an act of good faith, make a token payment to the Banaban people. Great Britain, Australia and New Zealand subsequently offered $A10 million, which was paid into a trust fund. The Banabans had also sought $11 million compensation for the replanting of land mined since 1913; BPC was only willing to offer $750 000. The Banabans took this matter to the court again, and ended up receiving a mere $11 000. This was a fraction of the millions the Banabans felt they deserved.

The central issue in this protracted court case, in the judge's opinion, had been the failure of the three governments to properly advise the Banaban people of the terms and conditions, and the consequences of the deal being made in 1947. So while Banabans won the court case on moral grounds, they did not reap the financial rewards they had hoped for.

At the end of the 1970s, a television documentary, international media coverage and the long court case had brought their problem on to the world stage. The question of Banaban resettlement and independence has still not been resolved.

ACTIVITIES

1 On a timeline, note down the events that took place on these dates: 1900; 1902; 1913; 1920; 1928; 1931; 1942; 1945; 1947; 1972–5; 1979.

2 Write answers to these questions.

- **a** What were the occupations of the first Europeans to visit Banaba?
- **b** Why did the Banaban population decline so drastically in the 1870s?
- **c** In two sentences describe what Banabans mean by land tenure.
- **d** In two sentences describe what Europeans mean by land tenure.
- **e** What percentage of phosphate payments was going to the Gilbert and Ellice Island Colony between 1900–79?

f What tactics did the Banabans use in the 1970s to achieve justice with the BPC, the British government and the Gilbert and Ellice Island Colony?
g Why did the judge in 1972–75 consider the 1947 deal so important?
h Why has Sir Arthur Grimble's reputation in Kiribati as everyone's 'favourite uncle' been challenged in recent years?
i What financial rewards did the Banabans achieve from their 1972–75 court case?

Land, chiefs, company and government

In 1900 a Banaban went on board *SS Archer* to meet Europeans and trade with shark fins, shark-tooth swords, fruit and vegetables. He was mistaken as the 'King' of Banaba by Albert Ellis who had come to investigate the possibility of phosphate mining. In the following weeks Albert Ellis found that there was not one king, but several chiefs. He obtained their signatures or signs, and these became the basis for the mining company's acquisition of land. Throughout the Pacific similar events occurred when chiefs or 'Kings' signed away land over which they had no control and which often belonged to individual landholders or communally to a whole village or community.

The link between government, chiefs, land sales and mining or plantation companies has occurred enough times for a pattern to be distinguished. For example, in 1905 the giant Colonial Sugar Refining Company (CSR), which held a monopoly over Fijian sugar production, wanted to develop 7000 acres of swampy land near Nausori. Government officials toured the area to convince the local people to lease the land to CSR for a low rental. The people refused. Local leaders (Fijian officials appointed by the government), Church officials and the local traditional Chiefs and High Chiefs tried to convince the people to rent the land. (The Chiefs received part of all land rentals.) The people pointed out that the swamp land, while not farmed, provided timber for building, firewood, crabs and eels, and leaves for weaving mats. This was one case when the partnership of company, government and Chiefs was unsuccessful.

In Papua New Guinea, in 1981, the government announced that mining lease negotiations with the giant American mining company Kennecott, could not be resolved satisfactorily. The government was unhappy with Kennecott's environmental safeguards and other land use problems. The proposed Ok Tedi gold and copper mine in the rugged, mountain ranges of the Fly River area appeared to have collapsed. Virtually overnight, after secret negotiations, the Papua New Guinea Government then announced that a new and acceptable mining lease had been signed with another company — Broken Hill Proprietary Limited (BHP) and a group of partners. Local landholders' rights had been protected. The government had put the local people's rights, and the benefit to the nation, before the profit margins and promises of an international mining company. This contrasts very dramatically with what happened on Banaba.

To establish their land rights and to protect their interests, Pacific Islanders now rely on consultants, environmental impact statements, lawyers and court cases. The Banabans, for example, went unsuccessfully to the United Nations in 1968, lobbied the Fijian government for support, and rather than a mass media campaign to embarrass their opponents, chose to appeal to a British court of law.

At the local level land issues today are more likely to involve a family dispute, hereditary rights or criticism of the role of Land Commissioners. Land disputes are a continuing feature of district, local and capital city courts in nearly all Pacific Island nations. The complicated issue of land rights is well illustrated in the division of forest plots on Kiebu Atoll in Kiribati (see Fig. 46).

The concern over land issues can be judged by a series of books recently published by the University of the South Pacific in Suva, Fiji. An old book, *Land Tenure in the Pacific*, originally published in 1971, was reprinted in 1977, and due to high demand was revised and republished in 1987. Books written by Pacific Islanders such as *Land Tenure and Rural Productivity* (1984), *The Politics of Land in Vanuatu* (1987), *Land Tenure in the Atolls* (1987) and *Land Rights of Pacific Women* (1986), continue to indicate the concern over land which is such an important part of life for 20th century Pacific Islanders.

ACTIVITIES

1 Go back to question 3 on p. 84. Check your list of demands. Add any new demands. Renumber your list in order of importance now that you know more about the Banaban issue.

2 Go back to question 4 on p. 84. Add any new information you now know.

3 List land rights issues in the Pacific which you know are still unresolved.

4 Write separate statements, of about 100 words each, for each of the following situations.
- ▲ a concluding statement for the judge in the 1972–75 Banaban court case
- ▲ a response to this statement from the BPC
- ▲ a response to this statement from the Banabans
- ▲ a response to this statement from the Gilbert and Ellice Island Colony government

Allow a partner to read all four statements, then ask your partner to give their own opinion on the events of 1972–75.

RESEARCH PROJECTS

1 Build up a folio of articles on Maori land rights in New Zealand.

2 Check with the mining companies like BHP, CRA or MIM about their mining policy and land rights at Ok Tedi, Pogera and Misima Island. This might be compared with the history of copper mining on Bougainville Island (see 'Bougainville copper', in *Current Affairs Bulletin* Vol 45/3, 1969).

3 Research the story of the Kanak people in New Caledonia and their efforts to protect their land rights.

4 Read Arthur Grimble, *A Pattern of Islands*.

5 Research the story of phosphate mining and independence on Nauru.

6 Compare the methods of passing on land rights from one generation to another. This comparison could include feudal England, Australian Aboriginal custom or socialist land policy in China or the USSR.

Resources

Bandler, F. *Treasure Islands: Trials of the Banabans*, Blond & Briggs, London, 1977.
Go Tell it to the Judge, BBC film, 1979.
Grimble, A. *A Pattern of Islands*, John Murray, London, 1952, pp. 1–54.
Macdonald, B. 'Grimble of the Gilbert Islands', in *More Pacific Island Portraits*, ed. D. Scarr, ANU Press, Canberra, 1978.
Macdonald, B. *Cinderellas of Empire*, Ch. 6, ANU Press, Canberra, 1982.
Macdonald, B. & Williams, M. *The Phosphateers*, Ch. 4, Melbourne University Press, 1985.
Silverman, M. *Disconcerting Issue: Meaning and Struggle in a Resettled Pacific Community*, University of Chicago Press, 1971.
Note that there are a number of articles on Banaba available in *Pacific Islands Monthly*, September 1976–November 1977.

GLOSSARY

Abortion termination of pregnancy in the womb, before birth

Annuities payment once a year (refers to mining payments for the use of a piece of land)

Archaeology the study of ancient 'dead' civilisations

Authentic real or true (not a copy)

Aviator an old word for aeroplane pilot

Beachcombers usually Europeans who temporarily lived 'island style' with Island people

Betray to tell a secret or give information to an enemy

Caldera wide depression left when the opening or crater of a giant volcano collapses during an explosion or eruption

Collaboration to help or work together with (refers to people who help an invading army)

Colony a country ruled by another nation

Combat zone area of fighting in a war, controlled by neither army

Conscription a way of obtaining workers (refers to villagers working for invading armies voluntarily or through force)

Crater opening or exit at the top of a vertical chimney of a volcano (As the volcano erupts this opening often collapses in or is blown apart, creating a wider opening or crater.)

Culture how people live: the pattern of all human life, including possessions, institutions, techniques, goals, rituals and beliefs

Curfew a time after which people must stay in their homes

Custom the usual (or traditional) way of doing things

Dig a place where archaeologists search underground for clues of ancient civilisations

Economic organisation how people arrange jobs to produce food, shelter and equipment

Fauna animal life

Flora plant life

Hereditary passed down from birth (refers to land ownership)

Horticulture the cultivating, tending and caring of land

Independence having control over your own affairs (refers to political power after colonial rulers have gone)

Indigenous a local person or language

Inexplicable cannot be easily explained or understood

Infamous famous for a bad deed

Infanticide to kill young babies (refers to a method of preventing overpopulation)

Initiation a ceremony to show a person has reached a certain age such as adulthood

Inter-marriage marrying someone from a different group (refers to marriage of people from different cultures)

Inventory a list of all items (refers to goods carried on a migration)

Kin family (refers to a large group who share a common ancestor)

Lava name given to very hot volcanic material once it escapes to the surface (It flows as moving molten rock until it cools down.)

Lease a piece of paper allowing temporary use (refers to permission to use or mine land)

Lifestyle the daily routine of human behaviour

Magma chamber huge underground cavity or cavern in which very hot material is contained until it finds a vent, crack or crater to explode out of

Magma name given to very hot volcanic material while it is still bottled up underground

Maritime to do with the sea (refers to a lifestyle based on fishing, trading and sailing)

Migration to move home from one location to another

Monopoly to have complete control, with no competition (refers to trading for shells, coconuts and timber)

Motif a pattern or feature (refers to pottery jars or pots)

Multinational giant companies with business in more than one country

Nomadic moving home regularly from one place to another

Perimeter the outside boundary of an area (refers to the edge of the territory which an invading army can claim they control)

Petition a list of complaints signed by a great many people and presented to a government or employer

Phosphate (guano) formed from lime, other minerals and bird droppings over millions of years

Posthumously to be given an award after death (refers to medals for bravery awarded to dead soldiers)

Precariously dangerously

Prehistoric ancient times before writing was used to record events

Profound having a very great impact

Provident fund when others put money away for your use to provide for you in the future

Province a region or part of a nation usually with its own government

Radio-carbon dating a method of giving a date to the remains of ancient bones, tools and rocks (based on the amount of radio-active carbon they lose each century as they age)

Re-enactment to perform exactly as before

Regime how things are done (refers to the period of colonial rule)

Replica an exact copy

Royalties payment based on a percentage of profits from each sale

Scrupulous taking great care (refers to correct payment of wages)

Squatters people who set up home where they have no legal right

Supernatural having powers greater than ordinary people (usually refers to gods or spirits)

Tenure land ownership (refers to permanent use of land)

Tephra ash which showers down from an erupting volcano

Topography the shape of the land (rivers, hills, valleys)

Tract usually refers to a large area of land

Tradition doing things as generations have done before

Trust fund to place your money in safe (trusty) hands, until it is needed for a special purpose

Uninhabitable not able to be lived on

Urbanisation the movement of people to cities (urban areas)

Volcanic cone a volcano which erupts through a vertical chimney developing a classical cone shape as ash and rock fall and build up around the chimney or crater

Vulcanology the study of volcanoes

Index

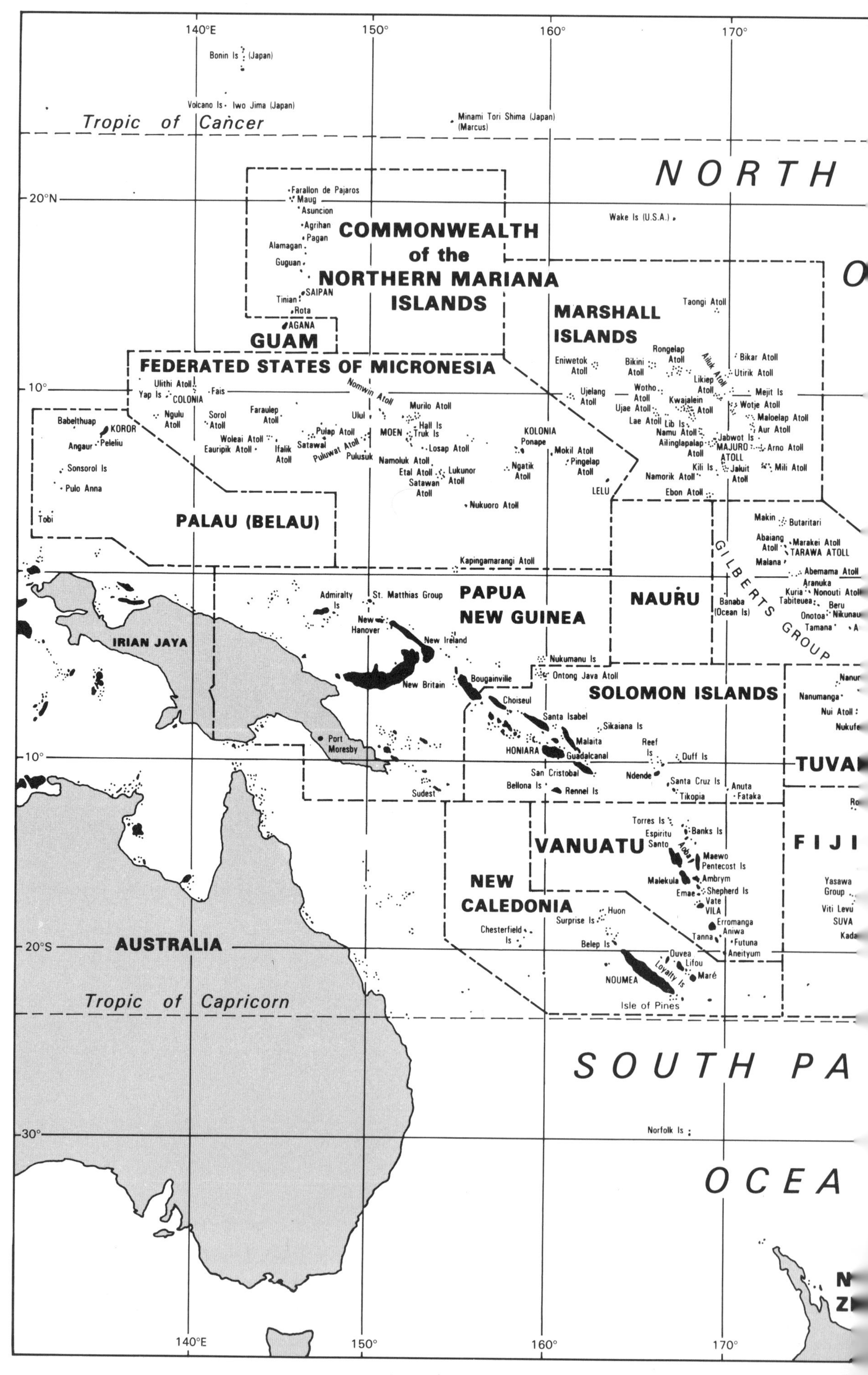

140°E
150°
160°
170°
Bonin Is (Japan)
Volcano Is
Iwo Jima (Japan)
Minami Tori Shima (Japan) (Marcus)
Tropic of Cancer
NORTH
20°N
Farallon de Pajaros
Maug
Asuncion
Agrihan
Pagan
Alamagan
Guguan
SAIPAN
Tinian
Rota
AGANA
COMMONWEALTH of the NORTHERN MARIANA ISLANDS
GUAM
Wake Is (U.S.A.)
MARSHALL ISLANDS
Taongi Atoll
Rongelap Atoll
Bikini Atoll
Eniwetok Atoll
Ailuk Atoll
Bikar Atoll
Utirik Atoll
Likiep Atoll
Mejit Is
Ujelang Atoll
Wotho Atoll
Kwajalein Atoll
Wotje Atoll
Ujae Atoll
Lae Atoll
Lib Is
Maloelap Atoll
Aur Atoll
Namu Atoll
Ailinglapalap Atoll
Jabwot Is
MAJURO ATOLL
Arno Atoll
Kili Is
Jaluit Atoll
Mili Atoll
Namorik Atoll
Ebon Atoll
FEDERATED STATES OF MICRONESIA
Ulithi Atoll
Yap Is
COLONIA
Fais
Nomwin Atoll
10°
Ngulu Atoll
Sorol Atoll
Faraulep Atoll
Murilo Atoll
Ulul
Hall Is
Truk Is
MOEN
Pulap Atoll
Woleai Atoll
Eauripik Atoll
Ifalik Atoll
Satawal
Puluwat Atoll
Pulusuk
Losap Atoll
Namoluk Atoll
Etal Atoll
Lukunor Atoll
Satawan Atoll
KOLONIA
Ponape
Mokil Atoll
Pingelap Atoll
Ngatik Atoll
LELU
Nukuoro Atoll
Babelthuap
KOROR
Angaur
Peleliu
Sonsorol Is
Pulo Anna
Tobi
PALAU (BELAU)
Kapingamarangi Atoll
Makin
Butaritari
Abaiang Atoll
Marakei Atoll
TARAWA ATOLL
Maiana
Abemama Atoll
Aranuka
Kuria
Nonouti Atoll
Tabiteuea
Beru
Onotoa
Nikunau
Tamana
GILBERTS GROUP
NAURU
Banaba (Ocean Is)
Admiralty Is
St. Matthias Group
PAPUA NEW GUINEA
New Hanover
New Ireland
IRIAN JAYA
Nukumanu Is
Ontong Java Atoll
New Britain
Bougainville
SOLOMON ISLANDS
Choiseul
Santa Isabel
Sikaiana Is
Malaita
Port Moresby
HONIARA
Guadalcanal
Reef Is
Duff Is
San Cristobal
Ndende
Santa Cruz Is
Anuta
Fataka
Tikopia
Bellona Is
Rennel Is
Sudest
Nanumanga
Nui Atoll
TUVALU
10°
Torres Is
Banks Is
Espiritu Santo
Aoba
VANUATU
Maewo
Pentecost Is
FIJI
Malekula
Ambrym
Emae
Shepherd Is
Vate
VILA
Yasawa Group
Viti Levu
SUVA
NEW CALEDONIA
Huon
Surprise Is
Erromanga
Aniwa
Chesterfield Is
Belep Is
Tanna
Futuna
Aneityum
20°S
AUSTRALIA
Ouvea
Lifou
Loyalty Is
Maré
NOUMEA
Isle of Pines
Tropic of Capricorn
SOUTH PA
30°
Norfolk Is
OCEA
140°E
150°
160°
170°